RHETORIC AND AMERICAN POETRY
OF THE EARLY NATIONAL PERIOD

by Gordon E. Bigelow

University of Florida Monographs
HUMANITIES
No. 4, Spring 1960

UNIVERSITY OF FLORIDA PRESS/GAINESVILLE, FLORIDA

EDITORIAL COMMITTEE

Humanities Monographs

T. WALTER HERBERT, *Chairman*
Professor of English

CLINTON ADAMS
Professor of Art

CHARLES W. MORRIS
Professor of Philosophy

C. A. ROBERTSON
Professor of English

MELVIN E. VALK
Associate Professor of German

PREFACE

Before the new recruit has worn his uniform long, he will encounter the advice, "never volunteer," which implies that he will find trouble enough in what he is required to do without exposing himself to more. That same advice should be given to any student of literature who attempts to say anything about the relationship of rhetoric to poetry. The safest thing for him is to stay away from the whole war, the next safest thing is to so limit his terms that no one can take exception. Most studies in this area do limit themselves to *elocutio* or stylistics, but I have violated that precaution by using a broader definition of rhetoric. I have adopted the classical conception of rhetoric as oratory, the art of persuasion, having five qualitative divisions of which *elocutio* is only one, and including the three major branches—deliberative, forensic, and epideictic. The concept of rhetoric here had to be inclusive because we are dealing with a large body of verse, some of which is rhetorical in some ways, some in other ways. It would have been convenient to limit the definition to deliberative or persuasive rhetoric, except that the epideictic branch, whose chief purposes are praise and blame and one of whose chief marks is ornate style, is of equal importance with the deliberative. I could not restrict the definition at this point without eliminating a large portion of the poetry with which the study attempts to deal.

It might also have reduced the task to deal only with oratory and not with rhetoric as theory, except that the poets of the early national period were involved with both and there is no easy way to separate the effect of one from the effect of the other on their verse. Because this generation of poets made no sharp distinction between the rhetorical and the poetic modes of discourse, rhetoric often infiltrated from within the literary tradition as well as through more obviously rhetorical channels, and while pointing this out I have made no attempt to distinguish one sort of rhetorical influence from the other in drawing conclusions.

I like to think of the concept of rhetoric adopted here as sane middle ground. Kenneth Burke conceives of it in much broader terms, as did George Campbell in the late eighteenth century. I have chosen the classical conception because it is not only sufficiently inclusive, but also sufficiently stable and widely known to serve as a useful standard. I have also felt it necessary to deal with the common pejorative meaning of rhetoric, which connotes bombast or excessively ornate style.

"Poetic" is taken to mean chiefly poetry, though in a broad sense which includes novels, short stories, or other writings which are belle-lettristic in their emphasis. This term will appear more stable than rhetoric because we start with a given body of writings which were offered by their authors and accepted by their readers as "poetry."

The main task of definition has been undertaken in Chapter 1, the most controversial portion of the study, though perhaps one of the most valuable. This chapter attempts a distinction between rhetoric and poetic as modes of discourse, an old and vexing problem which has been dealt with before, sometimes by critics of great eminence, but never very satisfactorily. Without expecting everyone to agree with the solution offered here, I will defend it because I am acquainted with no other which works as well in answering the questions raised by this study. Those who disagree will probably do so because they would like to adopt other concepts of rhetoric or of poetic. The distinctions made here probe into disputable areas involving the essential nature of rhetoric and poetic, where one can hardly walk without treading upon toes. Those who find this solution imprecise will probably find it possible to be more precise only by narrowing the scope included in the categories "rhetoric" and "poetic." One can draw sharper boundaries around smaller, more homogeneous areas. In all humility I offer this portion of the study as a challenge to someone else to turn up better working distinctions than those offered here.

The other limits of the study are quickly stated. The date 1775 was chosen as an initial point because it is a good approximation of the time when most poets writing in America considered themselves definitely Americans rather than British colonials. The terminal date 1815 indicates the approximate time when Bryant had finished his apprenticeship and was soon to publish *Thanatopsis,* with which the flood of more significant American poetry of the nineteenth century began. The period encompassed by these two dates, though nearly barren of poetry of great intrinsic worth, is nonetheless of importance to the literary historian and critic, for it witnessed the birth of many of our national tastes and ideals. It was a period of cultural as well as political and social ferment, in which a young America strove to assert her individuality in many fields of endeavor, and it was a time when rhetoric played an especially important part in American life. It has been, moreover, a period relatively neglected by literary scholars, and the present study, besides providing critical tools for working in a later period of higher literary importance, should shed light on some aspects of this interesting period in American literary history.

Except in Chapter 1 where I draw upon a rather diverse body of materials, I have concentrated on the poetry and the critical writings of the early national period, and a chart of my path is included in the bibliographical note at the end of the study. The poetry posed a problem: there was so much of it that to deal with the whole corpus would have been unwieldy, and the verse subjected to close scrutiny was limited to the writings of the poets thought most important by their contemporaries and those thought most important by posterity. These were Freneau, Barlow, Humphreys, Dwight, Trumbull, Hopkinson, and Robert Treat Paine. It seemed justifiable to concentrate on the poetry which represents the most serious attempts of the most capable poets to produce verse of high literary worth.

It is a pleasure to record my debt to Professor Charles R. Anderson, who wisely and patiently saw this study through in its original form as a doctoral dissertation at the Johns Hopkins University. My senior colleagues, Professors Frederick W. Conner, T. Walter Herbert, and Harry R. Warfel, generously read the manuscript and offered many helpful suggestions for its revision. Only one portion of this study has previously been printed. The first chapter, "Distinguishing Rhetoric from Poetic," was published in essentially its present form in the December, 1953, issue of *Southern Speech Journal.*

GORDON E. BIGELOW

GAINESVILLE, FLORIDA
MARCH, 1960

CONTENTS

1. DISTINGUISHING RHETORIC
FROM POETIC

During most of Western literary history, rhetoric and poetic have lain close together, sometimes merging so completely for centuries at a time as to be virtually indistinguishable. In the ancient world Aristotle was almost the only critic to make any thoroughgoing distinction between the two, and even this was more implicit than explicit in the simple fact of his having published both a *Rhetoric* and a *Poetics*. As C. S. Baldwin has shown, the nearly universal tendency of classical antiquity, especially in Rome where rhetoric came to dominate the whole of education, was to merge the two, with poetic commonly becoming subservient to rhetoric. "In the thought of Horace's circle," Baldwin writes, "the distinction between rhetoric and poetic as two movements, two ways of composing, seems to have been inactive. . . . Grammarians, rhetors, philosophers, men of letters seemed thus to converge under the Empire toward a poetic strongly tinged with rhetoric, no longer distinct as a movement having its own technique."[1] D. L. Clark has shown that this mixture of the two modes was inherited by the Middle Ages and that it persisted in England at least until the middle of the seventeenth century.[2] Essentially the same condition seems to have been true of the eighteenth century, though there is as yet no authoritative study.[3]

Real dissociation of rhetoric and poetic does not seem to have come about until the nineteenth century and the Romantic Movement, but here the break was sharp and deep. Romantic writers returned to a view of poetic discourse much like that of Aristotle, with renewed emphasis on its esthetic and pleasing qualities rather than on its moral and persuasive elements, though their poetic type was not the tragic drama which Aristotle had dwelt upon in the *Poetics*, but the personal lyric. The rebellion of the Romantic poets

1. *Ancient Rhetoric and Poetic* (New York, 1924), pp. 244-246.
2. *Rhetoric and Poetry in the Renaissance* (New York, 1922).
3. So distinguished a student of eighteenth-century literature as R. S. Crane finds Roman rhetoric to be the single most important shaping force on literary theory of the age. *Dictionary of World Literature*, ed. Joseph T. Shipley (New York, 1943), p. 195.

from the literary ideals and practices of the eighteenth century takes on new meaning when it is realized that what this rebellion amounted to in the main was a rejection of the rhetorico-poetic tradition stretching back some 1,500 years to late classical antiquity, a tradition which embraced nearly all of the great poets of Rome, of the Middle Ages, and of the English Renaissance. It is significant that Coleridge and other Romantic critics should derive their principles not from the Roman rhetoricians but from philosophic sources.

This long and close association of rhetoric and poetic renders any attempt to distinguish between them unusually difficult. Past attempts to define these two great modes of discourse and to discriminate between them have never been satisfactory for two chief reasons. First, critics have assumed that there are such things as "pure" rhetoric and "pure" poetry, whereas in practice there are few if any speeches which are not in some way poetic, or poems which are not in some way rhetorical. Second, critics have too often tried to capture the whole essence of a mode in a single definition and to oppose it to the whole essence of another mode without being aware that these modes are not simple but complex in nature, that they defy epitomization as wholes, and that they cannot be made mutually exclusive except on a special basis. For this reason most attempts to distinguish between the modes have screened out only certain classes of poems or speeches and have let others fall through the sieve. For example, John Stuart Mill's much quoted distinction between poetry and eloquence, "eloquence is *heard;* poetry is *overheard*,"[4] has this limitation, since it is based on a consideration of how the maker of discourse stands toward his audience, and neglects other considerations.

The approach I shall describe in the following pages involves two simple innovations: first, an assumption that absolute or categorical distinctions between the two modes cannot be made, but that the only real distinctions are relative ones—those of degree

---

4. "Thoughts on Poetry and its Varieties," in *Dissertations and Discussions* (New York, 1874), I, 96-97. Cf. Fred Newton Scott's formula for expressing the difference between prose and poetry: "Prose is expression for communication's sake; poetry is communication for expression's sake." "The Most Fundamental Differentia of Poetry and Prose," *PMLA*, XIX (1904), 263. The discussions of this problem of distinction which come closest to the approach outlined in this paper are by Bower Aly in "Rhetoric and Poetic," *Dictionary of World Literature*, and by Hoyt H. Hudson, "Rhetoric and Poetry," *Quarterly Journal of Speech Education*, X (April, 1924), 143-154.

or emphasis; second, that ordinarily no single distinction will serve, but that in each case a number of distinctions must be sought on various levels. These levels I have ascertained here by determining certain basic elements or conditions of discourse which both modes have in common. They are six in number: (1) a maker, (2) a purpose (which includes both a motive and a function), (3) an audience and an occasion, (4) a method, (5) a medium, and (6) a subject matter. It cannot be stressed too strongly that in the following analysis my intention is not so much to define rhetoric and poetic as to show how the two are most distinct from each other when considered in terms of the elements of discourse just listed. If someone were to gather up the distinctive characteristics of each mode as here set forth, he might be able to compile definitions of a sort, but they would be of unreal entities—a hypothetically "pure" rhetoric or a hypothetically "pure" poetry which exist rarely, if ever, in practice.

The element of purpose, since it governs to some degree the nature of most of the other elements of discourse, is perhaps the most useful means of distinguishing between the two modes and deserves first consideration. And since purpose is so intimately connected with "maker," I shall discuss the two together in a single section.

MAKER AND PURPOSE

The distinction between the two modes in terms of "maker" has been expressed most commonly in terms of the ancient adage: "Poeta nascitur, orator fit." Of course it would be foolish to take this completely at face value and claim that the orator is never a man of genius and the poet never anything *but* a genius. That is one reason why I have insisted that only relative and not absolute distinctions should be sought. Here, as at most of the other levels, the real distinctions are found to be a matter of degree or emphasis. Many critics have insisted that the truly great orator, like the truly great poet, must have a generous portion of natural talent or genius. But while the orator who was only competent has been accorded at least respect, the poet who was thought to be only competent has seldom received anything but scorn. The theoretical insistence that the poet be a man of genius has been nearly universal—even during times when reason has been accorded unusual respect, as in the English neoclassic period. Few critics have claimed that a

3

man could become a poet solely by learning the poetic craft from a textbook.

The basic assumption of rhetoricians has often been quite different, and the difference can be seen in the fact that the rhetoricians have produced innumerable manuals in which their art is reduced to a system so that it might be learned by any man of average gifts. While the elements of style—figures of speech, rhythm, grammar, syntax, and the rest—belong as much to the poet's art as to the orator's, it is significant that the manuals of style have been written not by poets but by rhetoricians and that they are called not "poetics" but "rhetorics." The ideal orator of antiquity, especially as described by Aristotle, Cicero, and Quintilian, was a man of the widest and most intensive learning and experience. Quintilian, for example, conceived of the whole of man's education from earliest infancy as being centered on the one aim of developing his capabilities as an orator. Yet only seldom in the *Institutio* are there suggestions that genius is an indispensable element in the orator.[5] The whole conception of the book works against this; it was intended to outline the ideal education for *all* Roman noblemen, and is permeated by the assumption that men of ordinary gifts, if they followed its teaching, could become at least competent orators.

The poet, on the other hand, has seldom been considered anything but the man of exceptional genius. In its extreme form, this view of the poet sees him as a kind of raving maniac, sometimes half divine, a man possessed and torn by the gift of prophecy over which he has little or no control. Plato sees the poet thus in the *Ion* and the *Phaedrus*,[6] and Aristotle said that "poetry demands a man with special gifts for it, or else one with a touch of madness in him,"[7] and that "poetry is a thing inspired."[8] Horace expresses

5. The Greeks apparently felt the same way. See R. C. Jebb, *The Attic Orators* (London, 1893), I, lxx: "In the Greek view, a man who speaks may, without necessarily having any first-rate natural gifts for eloquence . . . yet deserve to be distinguished from his fellows by the name of a speaker." Quintilian takes the common classical position that both art and nature are necessary to the best oratorical expression, but he seldom emphasizes nature. For one such passage, however, see *Institutio Oratoria*, trans. by H. B. Butler (London, 1932), II 19, 1-3.

6. *The Dialogues of Plato*, trans. Benjamin Jowett (London, 1892); *Ion*, 533; *Phaedrus*, 245.

7. *Aristotle's Art of Poetry* [*Poetics*], ed. W. Hamilton Fyfe (Oxford, 1940), XVII.

8. *The Rhetoric of Aristotle*, trans. Lane Cooper (New York, 1932), 1408b.

this vatic view in milder form: "I will take my name from the list of such as I allow to be poets. For you would not call it enough to round off a verse, nor would you count anyone a poet who writes, as I do, lines more akin to prose. If one has gifts inborn, if one has a soul divine and tongue of noble utterance, to such give the honor of that name."[9] Centuries later Sidney echoes this idea: "Onely the poet," he says, ". . . lifted up with the vigor of his own invention doth grow in effect into another nature."[10] He cites the Roman word for poet, *vates*, "which is as much as a diviner, foreseer, or Prophet."[11]

But there is no need here to insist on the extreme view; perhaps we need go no further than Wordsworth's more temperate remarks. Wordsworth thought that the poet differs from other men not so much in kind as in degree: "The poet is chiefly distinguished from other men by a greater promptness to think and feel without immediate external excitement, and a greater power in expressing such thoughts and feelings. . . ." He is a man "endowed with more lively sensibility, more enthusiasm and tenderness, who has a greater knowledge of human nature and a more comprehensive soul."[12] This is far from the Roman *vates*, but it still sees the poet as an exceptional man. The point, however, need not be argued at greater length. The poet, if the nearly unanimous opinion of the most thoughtful critics can be relied upon, may very well resemble the orator (or other men) in most ways, but he has something which sets him apart from other men—his genius.

To turn now to purpose. The purpose of rhetoric has most commonly been considered to be persuasion; this is twofold and involves a motive which is usually the desire of the maker to achieve some practical end, and a function which is usually to move men by means of persuasion to action in accordance with the desire of the maker.[13] An illustration might make this more concrete: a dictator

9. *Satires*, trans. H. Rushton Fairclough (London, 1929), I iv, 38-48.

10. Philip Sidney, "Defense of Poesie," *Works*, ed. Albert Feuillerat (London, 1923), III, 8.

11. *Ibid.*, p. 6.

12. "Preface to the Lyrical Ballads," *The Poetical Works of William Wordsworth*, ed. Thomas Hutchinson (Oxford, 1933), p. 937.

13. D. L. Clark sums up the general opinion of the ancient rhetoricians on the purpose of rhetoric as follows: "To the Greeks and Romans, rhetoric meant the theory of oratory. As a pedagogical mechanism it endeavored to teach students to persuade an audience. . . . Thus to the Greeks and Romans rhetoric was defined by its function of discovering means to persuasion." *Rhet-*

5

covets the fertile lands of a tiny neighboring country; he therefore directs his propaganda minister to prepare a campaign of radio addresses and newspaper articles to persuade his people that the tiny neighbor is planning to make war on them; influenced by these appeals, the dictator's people eventually act in accordance with his wishes and go to war. In this instance the motive which leads to the discourse is lust for power or for nationalistic expansion; the function of the various forms of discourse, written and spoken, is to provide the dictator's people with a good reason for attacking their neighbor. The motive is determined rationalistically, and the function is a quite practical one.

The motive and function of poetic discourse cannot be so easily specified. Samuel Johnson said that a man who wrote for any other reason than to make money was a fool. No doubt many poems and other literary works have been written to catch the eye and loosen the purse strings of some patron—be it a nobleman or the general public. And some literary works of great worth have been produced "on order," to celebrate a wedding or mourn a death. But it will hardly do to stop there and claim that all poets write because they must eat or must satisfy the demands of a patron. Too many, like Chatterton, have written in spite of hunger, and some, like Virgil or Lucretius, have written great verse who never had to worry at all about their next meal. The characteristic motive behind poetic discourse, and the motive which distinguishes it from rhetoric, is the "divine gift," the exceptional genius, the muse. It is not usually determined self-consciously or rationalistically like the motive of rhetoric; it is more apt to be innate, spontaneous, involuntary; the poet writes poetry because he is in some degree a "dedicated spirit." In poetic discourse, moreover, motive may be relatively independent of the function. One strong component of the poet's motive is simply that the discourse shall *be*, without reference to what it shall *do*. Many of the great poets—Dante, Spenser, Milton—conceived the end of poetry to be moral suasion, or the inculcation of religious or virtuous principles, a practical end simi-

---

oric and Poetry in the Renaissance, p. 6. While persuasion is the most characteristic purpose of rhetoric, it applies chiefly to the deliberative and forensic branches. Praise and blame have commonly been designated by the rhetoricians as the chief purposes of the epideictic branch, though these rarely exist without some admixture of persuasion. Even the so-called "new rhetoric" of Kenneth Burke has persuasion, or "identification" (Burke's more inclusive term) at its base. See *A Rhetoric of Motives* (New York, 1950), pp. 19 ff.

lar to that of rhetoric. But it was not this end which determined that their discourse should be mainly poetic rather than rhetorical; it was the "divine gift" which determined it.[14]

To turn now to the function of poetry, the other part of purpose. In brief terms, the distinctive function of poetry is to give esthetic pleasure rather than to persuade, to express or exhibit rather than to communicate. This is, however, an unlikely and theoretical extreme which should be modified to conform more nearly to actual practice. As W. S. Howell has shown, all poetry is in some degree communicative and in a sense persuasive, since no poem, if it is read with understanding, leaves a man exactly as it found him.[15] It might also be said, conversely, that many speeches give pleasure as well as persuade. Still there is a characteristic difference between the modes in their emphases on persuasion or pleasure. Rhetoric may propose both to please and to persuade, but the emphasis is on persuasion; poetry may also propose both to please and to persuade, but the emphasis is on pleasure. Horace's famous lines express this basic paradox concerning the function of poetry: "Poets desire either to profit or to delight, or to tell things which are at once pleasant and profitable."[16] Dryden, who oscillates between claims that pleasure is the chief end and that instruction is the chief end of poetry, states the typical compromise critics have made between these two: "Delight is the chief, if not the only end of poesy; instruction can be admitted but in the second place; for poesy only instructs as it delights."[17]

14. That the motive of poetic discourse is innate, spontaneous, involuntary, rather than rationalistic and deliberate, we can gather from the testimony of a number of poets. Shelley, for example, said that "Poetry is not, like reasoning, a power to be exerted according to the determination of the will. . . . The mind in creation is as a fading coal, which some invisible influence, like an inconstant wind, awakens to transitory brightness; this power arises from within . . . and the conscious portions of our natures are unprophetic either of its approach or its departure." Cf. Philip Sidney, "Defense of Poesie," *Works*, III, 36-37.

15. "Literature as an Enterprise in Communication," *Quarterly Journal of Speech*, XXXIII (1947), 417-426; see also Roland M. Frye, "Rhetoric and Poetry in Julius Caesar," *Quarterly Journal of Speech*, XXXVII (1950), 39-48.

16. *Ars Poetica*, lines 333-334.

17. "Defense of an Essay of Dramatic Poesy," *Essays of John Dryden*, ed. W. P. Ker (Oxford, 1926), I, 113. I am not unacquainted with the great mass of evidence which seems to militate against this view that the characteristic function of poetry is to give pleasure. Critics in the ancient world almost unanimously insisted on a didactic function for poetry; so did critics in the medieval world, and to a lesser extent so did critics in the Renaissance and

AUDIENCE AND OCCASION

Next to purpose, a consideration of audience and occasion is the most useful means of discriminating between rhetoric and poetic discourse. Rhetoric implies a specific audience and a specific occasion, both of which exert an immediate and important shaping influence on the nature of the discourse. According to Aristotle, it is the hearer who determines the speech. "The kinds of Rhetoric are three in number," he wrote, "corresponding to the three kinds of hearers to which speeches are addressed."[18] The orator, if he is to persuade successfully, must constantly be aware of his audience and must shape his discourse in accordance with his estimate of its effect on the audience. In a similar way, the orator's discourse is determined to an important degree by a specific occasion—the threat of an enemy invasion, the need for a higher tax, the prosecution of an accused criminal, the celebration of a great man's birth. Both audience and occasion tend to place fairly definite, even narrow, limits on the context of the discourse.[19]

If rhetoric is commonly designed for a specific audience and a specific occasion, it would be absurd to claim that poetry is written for no audience and for no occasion—though some poets and critics have suggested as much. Shelley said that "a poet is a nightingale who sits in darkness and sings to cheer his own solitude with sweet sounds"[20]—a typical overstatement which Shelley did not follow himself. Statements of this sort commonly go along with a strong belief in the vatic theory of poetic inspiration, and I am far from

---

neoclassic periods. But it should be remembered that during all this time rhetoric lay very close to poetry, sometimes edging so close for centuries at a time as to be virtually indistinguishable from it. I am inclined to believe with C. S. Baldwin that this general insistence upon a didactic function for poetry is the result of poetic acquiring a rhetorical characteristic. See his *Ancient Rhetoric and Poetic*, pp. 225, 240.

18. *Rhetoric*, 1358b. Cf. Burke, *A Rhetoric of Motives*, pp. 38-39.

19. Some speeches, of course, do have a more general audience and occasion. Isocrates' *Panegyric*, for example, a great piece of rhetoric which was reputedly written over a period of ten years, has an audience much more general than a group of men clustered about a speaker's rostrum, and an occasion much broader than a specific contemporary event. But it would be generally admitted, I think, that this piece in several important respects resembles poetic discourse more than it does rhetoric; and perhaps it should be mentioned that this "speech" belongs to epideictic oratory, which as a class tends to be closer to poetic discourse than the other two main branches of rhetoric.

20. *Defense of Poetry*.

insisting on that belief here. The poet, insofar as he seeks to communicate (and what poet who uses intelligible language does not?), is aware of some audience and some occasion, but these are both much broader than in rhetoric, and they exercise far less immediate control on the nature of the poet's discourse. The poet might speak to anybody, or as in some soliloquy to himself, or to nobody; he often appears to be speaking to all mankind and for all time. But neither audience nor occasion shapes his discourse except in a comparatively broad sense.

METHOD

The method of discourse is closely dependent upon the other elements of discourse, especially purpose. One of the basic laws of rhetoric, growing out of its purpose to persuade, is that the orator, before he employs other devices of persuasion, such as appeals to emotion, must first convince his audience of the reasonableness of what he is saying. Emotional appeals and ethical proofs have generally been considered among the most powerful means of persuasion, but it is usually presumed that they move within an orderly framework of facts and ideas.[21] The characteristic instrument of rhetoric, especially of deliberative and forensic rhetoric, is the enthymeme—the rhetorical syllogism—and the basis of persuasion is an enthymematic chain, by means of which the orator proceeds from one point to the next in establishing his argument.[22] The method of rhetoric, whatever recourse may be had to other means,

21. Longinus, for example, when discussing the orator's use of imagination, says that it introduces vigor and true feeling into a speech "when combined with practical arguments." *On the Sublime,* XV, trans. by A. H. Gilbert, in *Literary Criticism, Plato to Dryden* (New York, 1940). The ancient rhetoricians thought logic and orderly development important enough to make *dispositio* one of the chief qualitative divisions of rhetoric. Cf. the statement of D. C. Bryant: "Rhetoric, one way or another, has always run with logic. . . . There is nothing more than a good character which more persistently underlies . . . rhetorical teaching than the insistence upon intellectual processes in the speaker and intellectual content in the speech and the preparation of the speech." "Aspects of the Rhetorical Tradition," *Quarterly Journal of Speech,* XXVI (1950), 169-176.

22. Exception must be made to this in the case of some epideictic speeches, especially those in which display or virtuosity of expression is the end chiefly sought; but there are many speeches chiefly epideictic, like those of Isocrates, which also contain a strong deliberative element. These commonly show a deep concern for *dispositio* and make considerable use of enthymeme, example, and other persuasive devices.

is characteristically logical, a progression of ideas determined by reason and appealing chiefly to reason in the hearer.

Poetry has its own order and organization, but its method is different from rhetoric. For one thing, it is less rigorously logical and rationalistic; often its order is determined not so much by a chain of enthymemes in an argument as by a chain of events in a narrative, or by a sequence of associations, or by events or phenomena dependent upon a character or a theme idea. Aristotle conceived of the poet as primarily an "imitator," or a maker of plots, whose chief office was to imitate actions. This in essence would make of the poet a creator of life or a portrayer of life rather than, like the orator, an influencer of life. The poet's chief concern should be not with what is or what has been, but with what may be, and his method should involve an imaginative reconstruction of experience. The order of events for the poet is bound not so much to logic as to the necessities of plot and character.

Aristotle's remarks were attached to the tragic drama. Longinus also made interesting comments about the method of poetry, centering them not on drama but on one of Sappho's most intensely personal lyrics. He conceived of the characteristic method of poetry as selective and combining, a fusion of the most important elements of experience as opposed to the cumulation or amplification typical of oratory. He cited as an example how Sappho to portray the ecstasy of love chooses "the emotions that attend delirious passion from its accompaniments in actual life."[23] Her supreme poetic excellence is demonstrated by "the skill with which she binds together the most striking and vehement expressions of passion."[24] For Longinus the typical method of poetry was an imaginative realization of the most significant facts, which it combines or focuses or suggests in a flash. The method of oratory was amplification, a kind of extension or cumulation as opposed to the compression of poetry.[25]

John Stuart Mill also found the method of poetry to be alogical, dependent upon emotions rather than on reason. "What constitutes the poet is not the imagery, nor the thoughts, nor even the feelings, but the law according to which they are called up. He is a poet, not because he has ideas of any particular kind, but because the

23. *Longinus on the Sublime*, trans. by W. Rhys Roberts (Cambridge, 1907), X, 1.
24. *Ibid.*, XI, XII.
25. Cf. Baldwin, pp. 125-128.

10

succession of his ideas is subordinate to the course of his emotions." He then points out the difference between the function of emotion in the poet and in the orator. "In listening to an oration, or reading a written discourse, not professedly poetical, when do we begin to feel that the speaker or author is putting off the character of the orator or the prose-writer, and is passing into the poet? Not when he begins to show strong feeling; then we merely say, he is in earnest; he feels what he says; still less when he expresses himself in imagery; then, unless illustration be manifestly his sole object, we are apt to say, this is affectation. It is when the feeling . . . becomes itself the originator of another train of association, when it expels, or blends with, the former. . . ."[26]

In summary, the characteristic method of poetic discourse, unlike that of rhetoric, is essentially alogical, a movement from image to image determined by imagination or emotion, and appealing to imagination or emotion in the reader.[27]

Medium

Discrimination has often been made between rhetoric and poetic on the basis of whether prose or verse is the medium of expression employed, though this is one of the least dependable of criteria. Expression varies radically in accordance with changes in any of the other elements, especially that of purpose, and the medium of expression may be arbitrarily selected by the maker without reference to any of the other elements, or it may be chosen for him by convention. However, there remains little doubt that the customary medium of poetic discourse is verse, prose being suited to the practical purpose and logical method of rhetoric, and verse to the esthetic purpose and imaginative method of poetic discourse.[28] Although verse (i.e. regular metrical form, plus in modern times the added feature of rime) has been a chief means of distinguishing poetry from other discourse, many critics, including Aristotle, Cicero, and Quintilian, have observed that all verse is not necessarily poetry, indicating that they recognized the importance of other criteria in defining the nature of poetry. Aristotle pointed out that the his-

26. Mill, I, 116. See also Aristotle, *Poetics*, XVII, 2.
27. Cf. Baldwin, p. 134.
28. Within the last 150 years another distinction between the two modes has emerged, one which could hardly have been applied to earlier times; that is, that rhetoric is predominantly spoken, while poetry is predominantly written.

11

torian and the poet do not differ mainly because one writes prose and the other verse, for Herodotus' history could be put into verse and would still be history, not poetry. The historian, like the rhetorician, is mainly concerned with what has happened, the poet with what might happen; what chiefly distinguishes the poet is that he is an imitator, not a mere maker of meters.[29]

Aside from meter, extensive use of figures of speech has been considered more suited to poetic than to rhetorical discourse. Aristotle thought extravagant use of figurative language appropriate to poetry and inappropriate to rhetoric.[30] Cicero spoke of poets being more licensed to use "grand and figurative language," and of their having a "greater freedom in the formation and arrangement of words."[31] Quintilian repeatedly allowed freer use of figures to poetry than to rhetoric.[32] Longinus goes further and connects with purpose the use of figures in each mode. "You will be aware of the fact that an image has one purpose with the orators and another with the poets, and that the design of the poetical image is enthralment, of the rhetorical—vivid description."[33] "It is no doubt true," he added, "that those [images] found in the poets contain, as I said, a tendency to exaggeration in the way of the fabulous and that they transcend in every way the credible, but in oratorical imagery the best feature is always its reality and truth."[34]

SUBJECT MATTER

From one point of view little distinction can be made between the two modes in terms of subject matter, since speeches and poems alike may in theory utilize any topic within human knowledge and experience. Most attempts to make distinctions in such terms end up by considering other things, such as the poet's special gifts or the relationship of the maker to audience and occasion. Aristotle's statement, already quoted in another connection, is typical: the prose writer deals with facts, with what has been or what is, and the poet deals with idealized facts, with what may be. What this assertion implies is that the poet, because of his special gift, largely

29. *Poetics*, IX.
30. *Rhetoric*, 1405a-1408b.
31. *Orator*, trans. by H. M. Hubbell, (Cambridge, Mass., 1931), XX, 66-68.
32. *Institutio*, VIII, vi, 20, 35, 40, 44-59, 60-62, 68.
33. *On the Sublime*, trans. Roberts, XV, 2.
34. *Ibid.*, XV, 8.

12

creates his own subject matter, while the orator or historian takes that furnished him by the course of worldly events.[35]

An illuminating variation of this distinction between what is and what may be is provided by W. S. Howell. This variation, too, involves a consideration of audience and occasion. "Words which make up the rhetorical utterance lead the reader to states of reality, whereas the words making up the poetical utterance lead the reader to things which stand by deputy for states of reality. . . . Our transaction with rhetorical utterance is complete when we have fully connected its words with their referents. . . . Our problem in reading . . . any work of fiction or of poetry becomes that of finding the second set of references for its word."[36] Expository essays, speeches, and the like can, according to Howell, be called the literature of statement; poetry, drama, fiction, and the like can be called the literature of symbol. A simple illustration should make this clearer: Consider Milton's Satan addressing his host of rebel angels in Pandemonium. To the fallen angels, as they hear his speech, Satan's references to the burning lake, to the horrors of the battle just past, to God and to the Son are only too real; all are tangible and vivid elements of their immediate experience. Yet to us, who do not hear the actual speech but read it as an imaginative creation by a great poet, these references can be only symbols pointing the way to other referents somewhere in our own widely differing concepts and experience. To the fallen angels, who are in an essentially rhetorical situation with respect to Satan's speech, reason is quite enough to apprehend the full meaning of his words; to us, who are in an essentially poetic situation with respect to his speech, something else—perhaps imagination, perhaps Coleridge's "willing suspension of disbelief"—is also necessary.

One statement concerning subject matter might be made, though even this is a generalization to which there are many exceptions. In keeping with the practical purpose, the specific audience and occasion of rhetoric, rhetorical themes tend to be more limited in application than the themes of poetic discourse; and conversely, in keeping with the esthetic purpose and the more general audience

35. For two interesting variations of this by sixteenth-century Italian critics, see Mazzoni, "On the Defense of Comedy" in Gilbert, *op. cit.*, 360; and Castelvetro, "On the Poetics," *ibid.*, 305.

36. "Literature as an Enterprise in Communciation," *Quarterly Journal of Speech*, XXXIII (1947), 417-426.

and occasion of poetic discourse, poetic themes tend to be more timeless and universal than rhetorical themes.

In summary, I have insisted that no single distinction provides a net fine enough to sift out all of rhetoric from all of poetic, but that in judging the characteristics of any particular piece of discourse, a number of distinctions must be made on various levels, and that even on a particular level the differences between the two modes are not absolute but chiefly a matter of degree or emphasis. These criteria will be put to work in the ensuing chapters where the rhetorical elements of American poetry of the early national period are placed under close scrutiny.

2. FEEBLE POETRY
AND LUSTY RHETORIC

Freneau perceptively stated the literary spirit of his time when
he wrote that

> An age employed in edging steel
> Can no poetic raptures feel.[1]

Because it was the handmaiden of politics, most literature of the
early national period in prose or in verse was what we would today
call propaganda, a literature of polemic and invective, of exhortation
and persuasion. During the Revolution men of letters engaged in
a war of pens no less urgent and at times no less important than
the war of bullets. Even the ratification of the Constitution and
the formation of a true federal government brought with it no end
to controversy. Issues hotly contested in the dispute over the Constitution served to crystallize American politics into two parties
which were continually at each other's throats during the remainder
of the period. If guns and bullets were laid by after the surrender
of the British in 1783, heated words continued to fly with unabated
vigor. Poets and essayists who had defended the cause of liberty
during the Revolution took sides and fought with equal rancor in
the cause of the Federalists or the Republicans. In the 1790's party
issues were fanned to new heat by the French Revolution, which
split the country into Francophiles and Francophobes, and these
cleavages had hardly diminished before the War of 1812 brought
in a new wave of controversial issues and a new wave of polemics.
Such demands on literature to serve urgent, utilitarian ends forced
it to adopt attitudes and techniques which would be best suited
to those ends. These were, understandably, the attitudes and techniques of rhetoric.

It is true that there was no first-rate poetic talent in America at
this time, and this fact is sufficient to explain why there was so
little poetry of high worth, but it is also true that America did not
make the best of what she had. The main forces in American society, far from cherishing poetic genius, were hostile to it. The best

1. "To An Author," *The Poems of Philip Freneau*, ed. Fred L. Pattee
(Princeton, 1902-1907), II, 333.

minds were attracted to politics. Jefferson, Madison, John Adams, Hamilton, and Franklin—all wrote voluminously, but none thought of himself as a man of letters; certainly none had any intention of becoming a poet. Franklin remarked in his *Autobiography*, "I approved the amusing one's self with poetry now and then, so far as to improve one's language, but no farther."[2] Ezra Stiles, president of Yale from 1778 to 1795, showed how poetry was regarded in academic circles: "The lower branches of polite Literature I have an indifferent Opinion of; such as *Poetry*, the dramatic *Writings*, and the profusion of *modern Novels*."[3] He not only relegated poetry to "the lower branches of polite Literature," but he included oratory as a part of "the higher and more valuable branches." Nor was he the only college president who had a low opinion of poetry. John Witherspoon of Princeton had an interest in poetry which "was of the slightest, and the few poetic quotations he made in his lectures are used only to point some moral."[4] James Madison, a famous pupil of Witherspoon, held a similar view of poetry. He wrote to a young friend that poetry, wit, and criticism had captivated him as a young man, but that "something more durable befits a man of upper years."[5] Tom Paine wrote, "I had some turn, and I believe some talent for poetry, but this I rather repressed than encouraged, as leading too much into the field of the imagination"[6]—a remark not unfitting one whose most famous work is entitled *Common Sense*.

Coldness to poetry on the part of many of America's important men is only one sign that philosophical and religious attitudes of the day were unfriendly to poetry and friendly to rhetoric. I. W. Riley names five movements which dominated American thinking during the period: Puritanism, deism, Berkeleian idealism, French materialism, and realism or the common-sense philosophy.[7] In none of these does one find encouragement of the emotional intensity

2. *The Writings of Benjamin Franklin, Collected and Edited with a Life and Introduction*, ed. Albert Henry Smyth (New York, 1905), I, 270.

3. *The Literary Diary of Ezra Stiles [1769-1795]*, ed. Franklin B. Dexter (New York, 1901). The quoted passage is from a letter by Stiles to Mr. Tutor Lewis of Yale College, included by the editor under the entry in the diary dated February 16, 1775, I, 517.

4. Varnum L. Collins, *President Witherspoon, A Biography* (Princeton, 1925), II, 213.

5. *Poems of Philip Freneau*, I, lxix.

6. *The Writings of Thomas Paine*, ed. Moncure D. Conway (New York, 1894-1896), IV, 63.

7. *American Philosophy: The Early Schools* (New York, 1907), p. 10.

and imaginative insight which are necessary to poetic expression. The puritan clergy of New England, notoriously cool to the arts, constituted one of the most fecund literary groups. One contemporary critic said, "a larger portion of reputable American achievements in the field of authorship have been accomplished by persons of this profession than of any other in the United States,"[8] and another said that "the public is indebted to their exertions for a large proportion of our literary productions."[9] The Calvinists were especially prolific, growing more vociferous as their congregations dwindled.

Among the things they fought against was a growing rationalism which fostered the practical and useful in the realm of literature, where the only talents generally cultivated were those which could be turned to direct utility.[10] This meant that the writer should learn to write clear, simple prose, after the manner of Swift or Addison.[11] Joseph Dennie, editor of the *Port Folio*, found that "the coldness of our vast atmosphere soon chills" the infant poem.[12] Freneau found America to be hostile to the muses and mourned that reason was so strong that fancy could not survive.[13] He felt the time to be so hostile to poetry and so favorable to prose that he predicted a coming age in which common sense would make itself so strongly felt that prose would triumph completely over poetry.[14] His prediction was quite accurate; the Scottish "common-sense" philosophy became so influential that it has been considered the pre-eminently American philosophy.[15] Closely allied to this burgeoning of rationalistic thought was a growing interest in science and a commercialism so strong that Samuel Miller in 1803 could name it as one of the chief reasons for the inferior state of American literature.[16]

8. *The Monthly Magazine and American Review*, I (1799), 359.

9. *The Massachusetts Magazine*, VI (1794), 371.

10. J. H. Coberly found that "rather consistently, literature was given a functional character; a utilitarian motive was attached to the esthetic." "The Growth of Nationalism in American Literature, 1800-1815" (unpublished dissertation, George Washington University, 1949), p. 145.

11. One critic made the unusual claim that the study of oratory is the best way to achieve a good prose style. "Nothing contributes so much to polish the style as the cultivation of oratory." *Port Folio*, V (1805), 257. This claim was unique, however; other critics and rhetoricians advised the emulation of some great stylist, such as Addison, as the best means of acquiring a good style.

12. *Port Folio*, V (1805), 126.   13. *Poems of Philip Freneau*, II, 333.

14. *Ibid.*, III, 188.   15. Riley, *American Philosophy*, p. 477.

16. *A Brief Retrospect of the Eighteenth Century* (New York, 1803), I, 404-409. Similar reasons for the low state of American letters are given in an

There was also a lack of cultural facilities. The sophistication and leisure usually required to produce poetry had only feeble existence in the three or four largest cities. There were virtually no public libraries except for the beginnings of subscription library associations. Art galleries and museums were almost nonexistent except for the artistic activity at the Pennsylvania Academy of Fine Arts in Philadelphia and similar stirrings in New York and Boston. Even though literacy was widespread, especially in New England, it was for the most part bare literacy. The *Port Folio* stated in 1814 that one cause of the lowly condition of American literature was "the small number of persons among us whose minds have been disciplined by academical instruction," adding that law, politics, medicine, and the clergy absorbed all the highly trained minds in the country, leaving none for literature.[17]

There was a universal clamor for a great national literature, and this clamor involved a paradox: Americans called for a great national poet, but they were unwilling to buy enough books to support anyone who devoted himself to poetry. American inertia and indifference, as much as lack of international copyright laws, made it cheaper and safer for publishers to reprint the latest books by British authors of established reputation than to risk money on an unknown American. Anyone wishing to become the great national poet must be willing to starve in a garret—a price no American was willing to pay. There were two opinions as to what this national literature should be. The first, fostered by Federalists like Joseph Dennie, involved a reverence for things British. These men claimed that the way to attain native excellence was to emulate the British poets, especially Milton and the great Augustans, the greatness of the American product being measured in terms of its likeness to the original. The second opinion, held by many Democrats like Freneau, insisted that American literature should break completely with England and devise its own poetic method and use only American subject matter.

This hue and cry of nationalism had several damaging effects on

---

article in the *Monthly Magazine and American Review,* I (1799), 15-19. See also Daniel Webster's Phi Beta Kappa Address delivered at Dartmouth in 1809, *The Writings and Speeches of Daniel Webster* (Boston, 1903), XV, 576-581; and H. H. Clark, *Transactions of the Wisconsin Academy of Sciences, Arts, and Letters,* XXV (1930), 48.

17. II (1814), 45.

American literature. First, it created an urgent sense that a great poetry must be produced at any cost, lack of genius or other limitation notwithstanding; and it provided a strong motive for adopting the prescriptive methods of the British neoclassic poets. Second, nationalistic bias made critics in America either too lax or too strict in their judgment of American poems. One set of critics heaped extravagant praise on the sleaziest literary performance as long as it was American, accepting any bombastic, over-decorated sentiment or any versified commonplace as poetry. Another set, equally convinced that they were acting in the national interest, subjected American productions to the severest judgment based on the performance of the British poets. The one tended to cheapen the product and the other to deter prospective poets who feared public ridicule. Finally, nationalism resulted in a mass of poetry on patriotic themes, which was highly rhetorical.

A glance at the publishing scene tells the same story of esthetic sterility. One striking feature of publication was the large number of brief works in periodical or in pamphlet form. Charles Brockden Brown, the novelist, commented in 1806 that the United States was a land with few books but many publications, and added as if by way of extenuation that America was still "in a literary view, no more than a province of the British Empire."[18] Samuel Miller had been so impressed a few years earlier by the great preponderance of pamphlets and periodicals that he felt the century could be "emphatically called the age of periodical publications."[19] Among longer works the most successful kinds of publication were three: theological, political, and educational. A great many of the principal "authors" of the time were preachers publishing their sermons, or lawyers, teachers, politicians, and orators publishing their speeches. Aside from the reprints of English poets and novelists, only a small part of the total output of the presses was "literary." Out of thirty-eight works reviewed by C. B. Brown in the *Monthly Magazine* for 1799, *The Foresters, An American Tale* by Jeremy Belknap is the only American book which could be classified as literary. It is interesting that of the same thirty-eight works reviewed, thirty-one, or approximately four-fifths, were sermons or orations.

18. *American Register, or General Repository of History, Politics, and Science*, I (1806), 174.
19. *Brief Retrospect*, II, 246-247.

It is paradoxical that while there were virtually no professional poets, there were hundreds of poems. Samuel Miller, referring to both Europe and America, spoke of the eighteenth century as exceeding "all preceding periods with respect to the quantity of its poetry."[20] Dennie wrote in 1809 that among the pieces submitted to him for publication, poetry outnumbered prose ten to one. Most of the poetry, he added, was "scarcely less offensive than the compost heaps in a farmer's field."[21] C. B. Brown, at about the same time, found that "good poetry is the most scarce of all literary commodities, though poetry or matter that, by courtesy, bears the name is sufficiently abundant."[22] And in 1808 the editor of the *Monthly Anthology and Boston Review* spoke bitterly of being

harassed with a class of authors . . . [who] degrade the name, who are incomparably more numerous here . . . than in any other country. We allude to those who have triumphed over an audience in some species of occasional discourse, orations, sermons, etc., [or] who have occupied the poet's corner . . . those well-meaning men who have mistaken virtuous, patriotick sentiments in rhyme for poetic inspiration. . . .[23]

Since there were few versifiers who rose to the dignity of a volume, the greater part of this verse appeared in the poetry columns of the newspapers and periodicals.

Clearly poetry in America during the early national period was in a sad way. But if there was a scarcity of good poetry and of true poets, there was no lack of speechmakers; and if the age was hostile to poetry, it was more than friendly to oratory. Americans early acquired the reputation of being a speechmaking people. Some ten years before the Revolution, Soame Jenyns, the English poetaster and critic, objected facetiously to allowing American representatives in Parliament, because,

I have lately seen so many specimens of the great powers of speech of which these American gentlemen are possessed, that I should be afraid that the sudden importation of so much eloquence at once, would greatly endanger the safety and government of this country.[24]

20. *Ibid.*, p. 231.   21. *Port Folio*, new [3rd] series, II (1809), 597.
22. *American Register*, I (1807), 205.
23. *Monthly Anthology and Boston Review*, VIII (1808), 4-5.
24. *The Objections to the Taxation of Our American Colonies by the Legislature of Great Britain, Briefly Considered* (London, 1765), pp. 17-18,

Samuel L. Knapp's remarks in 1829 give some idea of the energy Americans devoted to becoming effective speakers:

No country has ever laboured harder to make orators than our own. In addition to fifty-three colleges, where classical educations are given, there are hundreds of minor institutions in which every rule of rhetorick is committed to memory; and every student can give you all the maxims from Blair, Campbell, and others necessary to make an orator; can tell you when to extend the arm, balance the body, raise the eyes, quicken the utterance, elevate the voice, and all the other golden rules to build up a Demosthenes or a Chatham. We have had most of the great dramatick actors from Europe to teach us. . . . Teachers have swarmed upon our shores and we have followed them and paid them extravagant sums for years.[25]

As might be expected, a great deal of the speechmaking centered in politics. Both national and local governments of the United States, with their democratic forms, placed a high premium on speaking ability. In a country where nearly every man was supposed to take some part in government, he almost literally had some "voice" in the government. Freedom of speech meant freedom to *make* speeches. To get elected to office a candidate had to electioneer, addressing as many of the voters as he could as often as possible; and once elected, he was expected to be effective in debate. But a citizen did not have to hold office to speak on political matters; much of local government was carried on through the debates and wrangling of ordinary folk.

Closely connected with politics was the profession of law. Bower Aly says of Americans in the early national period: "In spite of a native distrust of lawyers, they were perhaps as litigious as any people who ever lived. They busied themselves in the courts not only about such major crimes as murder, rape, and larceny but also about such petty matters as property lines, damage done by stock, and minor breaches of contract."[26] A chief qualification for any lawyer was an ability to speak effectively. Joel Barlow gave up the practice of law because "his oratorical powers were by no

---

quoted in M. C. Tyler, *The Literary History of the American Revolution* (New York, 1941), I, 84-85.

25. *Lectures on American Literature* (New York, 1829), p. 218.

26. William N. Brigance, ed., *A History and Criticism of American Public Address* (New York, 1943), I, 65.

means of a high order."[27] In 1794 C. B. Brown mentioned as qualities eminently subservient to the lawyer's purposes "a tunable voice, a fertile fancy, dexterity in argument, and promptitude in speech."[28] In a legal system where judges themselves were often barely literate in the law, where the court might be held in the common room of the local tavern, and where legal forms and etiquette, at least in the backwoods, might be reduced to informality, the decision of a case might rest upon the personality or the speaking ability of the lawyer.

A third great area for oratory was the church. Under the Puritan theocracy of New England, when the literary arts had been little encouraged, the art of pulpit oratory had been cultivated with a truly religious fervor. Preachers were trained to compose and deliver their sermons with careful skill, and audiences through long experience came not only to listen for the spiritual message, but to appreciate with real critical acumen the quality of the artistic performance.[29] By the end of the eighteenth century this tradition of pulpit eloquence was nearly two hundred years old in New England, and included such famous names as the Mathers and Jonathan Edward.[30] Even though the influence of the Puritan clergy waned during the century, there was no lessening in religious oratory, for as the strong current of Methodism and evangelical religion swept into America, a new and perhaps even more vigorous tradition of pulpit eloquence arose.

There were many forms of public diversion in which speechmaking was the central attraction. Fourth of July orations, funeral orations, and speeches on numerous other ceremonial or public

27. Samuel Kettell, *Specimens of American Poetry* (Boston, 1821), II, 4.

28. *The Rhapsodist and Other Uncollected Writings*, ed. Harry R. Warfel, in *Scholars Facsimiles and Reprints* (New York, 1943), p. 108.

29. For scholarly discussion of pulpit oratory in seventeenth-century England, which had close relation to the American tradition, see Caroline F. Richardson, *English Preachers and Preachings, 1640-1670: A Secular Study* (London, 1928); and especially W. Fraser Mitchell, *English Pulpit Oratory from Andrewes to Tillotson: A Study of Its Literary Aspects* (London, 1932). For the effect of pulpit oratory on American prose style of the eighteenth century, see Howard M. Jones, "American Prose Style: 1700-1770," *Huntington Library Bulletin*, No. 6 (November, 1943), 115-151, reprinted in Jones, *Ideas in America* (Cambridge, Mass., 1944), pp. 70-106.

30. Cf. Bower Aly's comments in Brigance, *American Public Address*, I, 82-83. Chapter 11 of Perry Miller, *The New England Mind* (New York, 1939) provides an excellent discussion of rhetoric in seventeenth-century New England.

occasions were nearly always assured of full and appreciative audiences. There were so many orations given on every conceivable public occasion that speakers often resorted to hackneyed formulae or took to outlandish bombast in a wish to be original.[31] Public dinners were apt to include, in addition to orations, long sequences of toasts accompanied by appropriate responses, cheers, and flourishes from a brass band.[32] Some persons were so willing to listen to speeches that they would sit through hour-long orations in Latin, Greek, or Hebrew at college commencement programs. These graduation exercises in the college towns were another form of public amusement indulged in by the parents of members of the senior class and by townsfolk of all ranks and conditions as well.[33] They customarily lasted from early morning to late afternoon and included such a formidable number of speeches and rhetorical displays that one wonders at the fortitude of the audience.

But any discussion of the oratory of this period which attempts to classify speeches by occasions is likely to give the false impression that Americans spoke only on occasion. The fact is, as Bower Aly says,

Speechmaking went on in the daily exercises of life in situations and under conditions that defy classification. And if no situation requiring speechmaking was at hand, then one was invented. The literary society, the "bee," the debating society and the lyceum were largely given over to speechmaking in one form or another.[34]

With so great a demand for speakers, it was only natural that rhetoric should be an important study in the colleges. Varnum Collins remarks in his biography of President Witherspoon of Princeton that "the part . . . oratory played in the daily life of the College was preponderant. . . . Oratory and the classics had been the backbone of the Princeton curriculum when President Witherspoon arrived, and he left oratory even more firmly entrenched."[35] Rhetoric had

31. *Monthly Anthology*, II (1805), 319. One of the fullest and most informative accounts of speechmaking during this period appears in the *Monthly Magazine*, I (1799), 241-244.

32. See for example the long sequence of toasts from the *Missouri Gazette and Public Advertiser*, July 12, 1820, reprinted in Brigance, I, 86-88.

33. For the program at the Yale commencement in 1781, see *Diary of Ezra Stiles*, II, 554-555.

34. In Brigance, I, 89.

35. II, 155, 209. For a thorough study of one phase of oratory at Princeton, see Ruth E. P. Paden, "The Theory and Practice of Disputation at Princeton,

always been a part of the curriculum in the colonial colleges, but until the middle of the eighteenth century it had been pursued mainly in Latin and centered chiefly in the works of Peter Ramus and his disciples, Talaeus and Dugard, who considered rhetoric an auxiliary to the science of logic, a matter of style and ornamentation. After 1750 a number of important changes occurred: English replaced Latin; the great classical rhetoricians replaced Ramus; and a split occurred between the written and spoken phases of rhetorical study, with "elocution," or the science of delivery, receiving more and more emphasis, and written rhetoric coming to be more closely identified with criticism, belles-lettres, and the general arts of literature.[36] This split resulted in more time and attention, rather than less, being devoted to rhetorical studies, since instead of one there were now two courses of study in which rhetorical principles were emphasized. It also meant that poetry was lumped with grammar and syntax in a program usually based on the ancient rhetoricians. Poetry in such circumstances tended to become a technique which could, like grammar or syntax, be mastered by anyone who followed the prescribed rules.[37]

Columbia, and the University of Pennsylvania, from 1750-1800" (unpublished dissertation, University of Iowa, 1944). See also Ota Thomas, "The Theory and Practice of Disputation at Yale, Harvard, and Dartmouth from 1750-1800" (unpublished dissertation, University of Iowa, 1942). For a more general treatment of the subject by Thomas, see Brigance, Vol. I, Chapter 5. Useful discussions of the college curriculum in early American colleges include Colyer Meriwether, *Our Colonial Curriculum, 1607-1776* (Washington, 1907); Louis F. Snow, *The College Curriculum in the United States*, in *Columbia University Contributions to Education*, No. 10 (New York, 1907). Other studies of oratory in early American colleges include: David Potter, *Debating in the Colonial Chartered Colleges, An Historical Survey, 1642-1900*, in *Columbia University Contributions to Education*, No. 899 (New York, 1944); Mary M. Robb, *Oral Interpretation of Literature in American Colleges and Universities* (New York, 1941), pp. 19-70; and Donald Hayworth, "The Development of the Training of Public Speakers in America," *Quarterly Journal of Speech*, XIV (1928), 489-502.

36. For much of the information on rhetorical theory in American colleges I am indebted to Warren A. Guthrie's excellent study, "The Development of Rhetorical Theory in America, 1635-1850" (unpublished dissertation, Northwestern University, 1940); published in reduced form in *Speech Monographs*, XIII (1946), 14-22; XIV (1947), 38-54; XV (1948), 59-71.

37. A. R. Humphreys shows in a suggestive article that many of the rhetorical characteristics in British neoclassic poetry are traceable to the almost universal practice in the grammar schools of writing Latin poetry as a literary exercise. "A Classical Education and Eighteenth Century Poetry," *Scrutiny*, VIII (1939), 193-207.

24

Cicero continued to be a part of the regular training, both the *Orations* and the *De Oratore* being translated methodically day by day. Much of Demosthenes and Quintilian was absorbed in the same way. One important phase of speechmaking in the early colleges consisted in formal disputations in Latin, which dealt with subjects like those with which Milton had wrestled in the Prolusions: "Whether day is more excellent than night," "Is mankind advancing to a state of perfectability?" "Are all mankind descended from one pair?" By 1800 disputations had been replaced by other exercises, such as forensic debates, with every student required to take part several times a year, in some instances once a month. In addition to this, each class gathered in the chambers of its tutor at least one morning a week to declaim prepared speeches which usually were memorized excerpts from famous English and American orations or selections from the standard English poets. A student of poetic bent might compose a poem of his own to be delivered before the class at such times.[38]

Students pursued rhetorical studies not only in school but during leisure hours as well. The "literary" societies may have been more influential in developing speaking ability than the formal studies. John Blair Linn wrote in 1795 that "the benefits which youth receive from societies established for literary purposes are considerable. There are so many institutions formed from this motive now existing that the love of them seems to be prevalent in the breast of every youth. . . . The particular objects which these societies pursue are composition, verbal debates, and oratory."[39] These societies usually went in pairs, originally differentiated by their political views. At Princeton there were the American Whig and the Cliosophic societies, at Harvard the Hasty Pudding and the Speaking clubs, and between these campus groups there was as lively a spirit of rivalry as between party groups in the national political scene. By the 1790's most of the political coloring of these societies had disappeared, though rivalry, based now on fraternity spirit, remained as keen as ever.[40] Many of the peculiar characteristics of

38. For a "poetic" account of the schoolboy orator, see George E. Hastings, *The Life and Works of Francis Hopkinson* (Chicago, 1926), p. 84. For another glimpse of such speechmaking see Francis Hopkinson, *Miscellaneous Essays and Occasional Writings* (Philadelphia, 1792), II, 35.

39. *Miscellaneous Works, Prose and Poetical* (New York, 1795), pp. 39-42.

40. For discussions of the literary societies see Jacob N. Beam, *The American Whig Society of Princeton University* (Princeton, 1933), especially pp. 126-

these societies sprang from this attitude of rivalry. Each organization, jealous of its prestige and reputation, saw to it that whenever a member made a public appearance he reflected only credit on his society. In the secrecy of the society's rooms he underwent a rigorous training in all phases of composing and delivering speeches, from grammar and spelling to the niceties of gesture. Essays, poems, and humorous pieces were often submitted anonymously to an official reader to be read aloud at meetings. The importance of these literary societies in training speakers and writers in America during this period can hardly be exaggerated, and it is of especial interest to note that poetry and oratory were mixed in these activities, just as they had been mixed in curricular studies.

In the world outside the schools there were as many encouragements for the orator as there were discouragements for the poet, an effective speaker being virtually assured of success in that world. As one contemporary critic said: "The true ambition of a man of genius and of high aspiring mind . . . is to be an orator. It has been correctly remarked that in such a government as ours oratory is synonymous with wealth and fame and civic honours."[41] Oratory was as suited to the tenor of American life during this period as poetry was unsuited, and if Americans felt inferior and provincial toward Britain in the matter of poetry and the other arts, they had no such feeling about their oratory. The periodicals are full of prideful comments about the great number and the excellence of American orators: "The nation at large is characterized by a greater aptitude for public speaking, more generally diffused, and more frequently displayed in flights of bold, nervous, and beautiful eloquence than any other that now exists—and, ancient Greece per-

---

141; and Edward B. Coe, "The Literary Societies," *Yale College*, ed. William L. Kingsley (New York, 1879). See also Charles E. Cunningham, *Timothy Dwight* (New York, 1942), pp. 248-252, for the severe restrictions on the use of the college library by undergraduates. For an excellent contemporary summary of rhetorical training in American colleges see *Port Folio*, new [3rd] series, II (1809), 99.

41. *Port Folio*, new [3rd] series, VI (1811), 217. Cf. John Blair Linn's comments: "Of the importance of oratory we need but slightly hint, for it is daily exemplified at the bar, in the pulpit, and in the senate. It is this which so much sways the passions of men, one while making them feel a soldier's warmth, and now the soft emotion of sympathy. Do any of us wish to serve our country in the cabinet or even in the field? This then is an essential study." *Miscellaneous Works*, p. 27.

haps excepted . . . that ever did exist."[42] One writer, impressed by America's excellence in oratory and her mediocrity in the other arts, recommended that all other arts should be set aside in favor of oratory:

Eloquence seems to flourish well among us. Let us therefore encourage its growth till it becomes the distinguishing feature of the American people. Let us, since we are excluded from many of the means which advance the glory of a nation, endeavor to exalt our fame by excelling in one of the noblest qualities of our nature.

Like a polished republick of antiquity, we will be content to be characterized by our commerce and our oratory. The winds which waft the redundant products of our industry to the remotest regions may also bear our renown as the most eloquent people of the earth.[43]

42. *Port Folio,* new [3rd] series, V (1811), 391. For similar comments on the excellence of American oratory see *Port Folio,* new [3rd] series, II (1809), 23-24; IV (1810), 216; VI (1811), 589; 3rd [i.e., 4th] series, IV (1814), 56; V (1815), 175-176, 297-298; and *Monthly Anthology,* VI (1809), 382; VII (1809), 148.
43. *Monthly Anthology,* II (1806), 502-503.

27

3. CLOSE ALLIANCE OF
RHETORIC AND POETIC

Not only must the booming voice of the omnipresent orator be reckoned with, but also the quiet sibilance of rhetorical precept whispering from within the literary tradition. This second voice was lent considerable power in shaping American poetry because both poets and critics failed to make more than the most superficial distinctions between rhetoric and poetic as modes of discourse. Because there was very little in the feeble poetic of the time to resist the encroachments of a lusty and burgeoning rhetoric, the boundary between the two became indistinct. As rhetoric washed into the semivacuum left by the absence of a strong poetic, speeches came to be an accepted vehicle for nearly all literary purposes— including the presentation of poetry, if one can judge from the extraordinary number of poems written to be declaimed before an audience. The function of the poet and the orator tended to fuse, and it is difficult to say today whether the works of such men as Robert Treat Paine are more properly described as declamatory poems or poetic orations. The after-dinner poet came to be as standard a fixture at public celebrations as the orator himself, and commonly their performances were distinguishable only because the poet's speech was in verse.

America had no live poetic tradition, but she did have a vigorous and time-honored tradition of oratory. Because people at this time were far more capable of appreciating a fine speech than they were of appreciating poetry of any kind, it is not unnatural that poetasters like Robert Treat Paine should appeal to their public in the manner which was most attractive to them. But it is damning evidence of the deficient poetic taste of the time that Paine should be hailed as a great poet, and it clearly illustrates how far rhetoric had come to dominate public taste in literature.[1] Speeches seem to have been

1. Just how highly Bostonians in the last decade of the eighteenth century regarded Paine's poetic talents can be seen by the high prices he was paid for his poetry, and by the great demand for his pieces. For his poem entitled "The Invention of Letters," for example, he received $1,500 exclusive of expenses, and for his "Ruling Passion" a clear profit of over $1,200. *The Works in Prose and Verse of Robert Treat Paine Jun. Esq.* (Boston, 1812), p. xiv.

composed as much for print as for oral delivery, often being equipped with long and numerous footnotes. Critics tended to treat speeches like any other composition, calling them to account for style, diction, and even punctuation. None of this is new in the history of literature. The close relationship between the spoken and the written word in America during this period is analogous to conditions in Greek and Roman antiquity. Orations had constituted a chief literary genre in the sophistic periods of antiquity—periods with which the early Americans were closely familiar through their rhetorical schooling. The word "speech" to designate a legitimate literary form was surrounded for them by all the prestige attached to the works of Isocrates, Demosthenes, and Cicero. This emphasis upon oratory as a "fine art" did not result in America, as it had in ancient Rome, from a suppression of the functional modes of oratory by an arbitrary act of government. In Rome oratory had necessarily turned to an emphasis on style because this had been its only means of survival. In America during the early national period what could be called a "later sophistic" came about because of an extension of functional oratory and not a curtailment. There was every encouragement in America to the practical modes of oratory, and the orator as artist or entertainer was at first an appendage to the orator as the effective manipulator of public opinion. The orator-artist arose in America as the result of a cultural need and of the universal cultivation of oratorical techniques which had only to be adapted to fill that need.[2]

Not all observers were content with the state of affairs in American literature, however, and some placed blame for the low state of literature squarely on the vogue for oratory. The *Port Folio* in 1814 blamed the decadence of American literature on

the great prevalence of public speaking, both from the number of our political and religious meetings, and the multitude of our courts of justice. This very frequent exercise of oratorical talents, a natural consequence of our form of government, not only occasions eloquence to be more cultivated and in higher esteem but imparts a declamatory style to our writers. In fact the greater part of our authors are also public speakers, and where they are not, they follow the reigning humor, and strive to write beautifully, and eloquently

2. Much more will be said in Chapters 5 and 6 concerning the large body of epideictic poetry which was one of the chief stocks in trade of these orator-artists.

and pathetically, in which attempt they insensibly fall into mere rant and declamation (II, 192-198).

Undoubtedly the elocutionary training in the schools and colleges helped to confirm the close relationship of rhetoric and poetry. As exercises for this training in the art of "reading" (i.e., in the technique of oral delivery), extracts from poems, essays, or speeches were used indiscriminately. The plan of James Burgh's *Art of Speaking*[3] was followed by most elocution manuals. This book begins with a brief essay "in which are given the rules for expressing properly the principal passions and humours, which occur in reading or public speaking," followed by the major portion of the book, consisting of "lessons taken from the ancients and moderns." In the prefatory essay, each of the major passions is listed and its main characteristics described; e.g., "Malice, or spite, sets the jaws, or gnashes with the teeth; sends blasting flashes from the eyes; draws the mouth toward the ears; clenches both fists, and bends the elbows in a straining manner. . . ." The poetry serving as lesson exercises was then printed with marginal labels suggesting the emotion which the reader should attempt to represent for each part of the poem. Here is a portion of Burgh's reprint of Adam's address to Eve from Book IV of *Paradise Lost*. The italicized words are supposed to receive especial emphasis:

Awe	*Sole partner,* and *sole part* of *all* these *joys*
Tenderness	*Dearer thyself* than *all. Needs* must the *pow'r,*
Pity	That *made* us, and for us this *ample world,*
	Be *infinitely good,* and his good
	As *liberal* and *free,* as *infinite;*
Gratitude	That *rais'd* us from the *dust,* and *plac'd* us *here*
	In *all* this *happiness.*[4]

And a passage from Ambrose Phillips' "A Lovesick Shepherd's Complaint":

Lamentation	Ah *well-a-day!* how long must I endure
	This *pining pain?* (1) or *who* shall speed my *cure?*
Anguish	Fond love *no cure* will have; seeks *no repose;*

3. Published in London in 1761. The edition used in the present study was printed in Baltimore, 1804. For a discussion of the most important readers used in America and of the elocution movement in America during this period, including analyses of the chief elocutionary texts, see Guthrie, "The Development of Rhetorical Theory in America," pp. 189-196, 223 ff.

4. Burgh, p. 162.

	Delights in *grief,* nor *any measure* knows.
Complaint	(2) Lo! now the moon begins in clouds to rise,
	The bright'ning stars bespangle all the skies.[5]

(1) The words pining pain cannot be spoken too slowly.
(2) These lines are to be spoken slowly and with a torpid uniformity of tone.

Burgh's method becomes clear from these extracts. The student should not simply recite the lines, but should act them out according to the marginal suggestions. The speaker's whole body shared the discipline—the head, arms, legs, hands, and face each performed its part according to the prescribed formulae. After such training as this, a considerable amount of which every schoolboy received, it should not be surprising that histrionic gesture and bombast were connected to poetry by strong bonds.

This blending of rhetoric and poetic in practice was taken for granted in the literary criticism, and although there are few direct statements by poets and critics identifying the two, there are other signs of the theoretical fusion. The blending was implicit in the chief sources from which Americans of this period derived their poetic and esthetic ideals, all of which sources were, roughly speaking, classical. The most important of these was the neoclassic tradition inherited from England, which made itself felt in the literature chiefly through emulation by Americans of the poetic practice of the great Augustan poets, and through widespread adoption of the works of the Scottish rhetoricians, especially Kames and Blair. There was considerable independent study of the ancients who still served as the basis of the educational system, especially Horace, Cicero, and Quintilian. Such direct knowledge of the ancients created no conflict with the reigning authority of the Scots, whose writings were, after all, pridefully anchored in the classical poets and rhetoricians.

Among the English Augustans, Dryden and Pope were the most admired and the most frequently emulated by Americans. The poetry of both contains important rhetorical elements. Mark Van Doren, whose critical analysis of Dryden is perhaps one of the most authoritative and the most sympathetic, says that

It was not until Dryden's time, when the inspiration of the Elizabethans had in a way given out, and the full body of modern classi-

5. *Ibid.,* p. 71.

31

cal doctrine was being received in its most systematic form from France, that eloquence came to feel completely at home in poetry ... Dryden was peculiarly fitted to lead the rhetorical grand march in English poetry. Possessing all of Ovid's fondness for exhortation and pleading, he possessed in addition unexampled power of classifying and dividing his thoughts, hitting upon happy generalities, thumping out bold new epithets, and accumulating stores of rhetorical energy. . . . He carried eloquence as high as it can go in poetry.[6]

Elder Olson has demonstrated that some of the chief characteristics of Pope's poetry are those of rhetoric rather than poetic. He finds it curious that critics have not assumed that Pope is a rhetorician and attempted to explain his works in the light of rhetorical rather than poetical principles. "The absence of this assumption," he says, "seems especially curious when we observe that the greater portion of Pope's work, if we set aside the translations, is either satire or didactic, and that satire and didactic, as invariably involving a consideration of audience, would fall not under poetics, but under rhetoric." He shows that Pope's own critical doctrines "were derived from men who either were rhetoricians, or who sought, in their writings, what was primarily a rhetorical end."[7]

Americans in the late eighteenth century did not fail to note the affinities of Pope's poetry to rhetoric, and according to Agnes Sibley this is one of the chief reasons why he was so highly esteemed in America. "They appreciated the close relationship between rhetoric and morality. They believed that true oratory and poetry teach men the way to virtue; and conversely, that instruction is most effective when given in the form of persuasion which poetry and oratory adopt."[8] She demonstrates that Pope's poetry was used in the grammars and rhetorical textbooks to illustrate figures of speech or points of grammatical usage or to provide exercise material for students' practice in declamation and oral recitation of verse.

Among the Scottish rhetoricians, Lord Kames with his *Elements of Criticism* (1762), Hugh Blair with his *Lectures on Rhetoric and Belles Lettres* (1783), and George Campbell with his *Philosophy of Rhetoric* (1776) are of the greatest significance to this study.[9] Kames'

6. *John Dryden* (New York, 1946), pp. 46-47.
7. "Rhetoric and the Appreciation of Pope," *MP*, XXXVII (1939), 13-35.
8. *Alexander Pope's Prestige in America, 1725-1835* (New York, 1949), p. 73.
9. For the influence of the Scots on literary theory, see William Charvat, *Origins of American Critical Thought, 1810-1835* (Philadelphia, 1936). For

32

book was not, strictly speaking, a rhetoric at all, but a systematic attempt to investigate the principles of the fine arts, and his treatment of literary phenomena is of less importance than his delineation of esthetic principles. His influence was strongest during the early years of the period, but after 1790 he was somewhat overshadowed, though by no means replaced, by Blair.

It was not until after 1785 that Blair's *Lectures* began to exert strong influence in America, but from 1790 on it was the dominant work in the field of rhetorical and literary study until after the Civil War. Blair was much indebted to Kames not only for his basic approach to literary and rhetorical study, but also in many other respects.[10] Because of an extremely close relationship between the two books, the following discussion of Blair can also represent the position of Kames.[11]

Some idea of the theoretical fusion of rhetoric and poetic discourse in Blair can be gathered from the title of his book, though a search for his specific statements as to their oneness is disappointing. His confusion of the two modes appears not so much in what he says about their relationship as in what he implies in his discussion of other things. That he recognized the problem is plain from the following: "It is hardly possible to determine where eloquence ends and poetry begins; nor is there any occasion for being very precise about the boundaries as long as the nature of each is understood."[12] But poetry and eloquence for him had much in common.

---

their influence on the theory and practice of oratory, see Guthrie. The influence of Kames on Trumbull, Dwight, and Barlow has been discussed at some length by Leon Howard in *The Connecticut Wits* (Chicago, 1943).

10. Guthrie, p. 83. Blair's famous book was first published in 1783, though the lectures contained therein had been delivered at the University of Edinburgh during the previous twenty-four years. Guthrie notes that the book was ordered by Brown University in 1783 and that the first American edition appeared in Philadelphia in 1784. Some idea of its popularity can be surmised from the following list of some of the American printings during the period: 1789, 1793, 1797, 1798, 1802, 1803, 1804, 1805, 1807, 1809, 1812, 1815, 1817. Guthrie claims (pp. 84-85) that by 1803 it had been adopted as a text by nearly all American colleges.

11. See Helen W. Randall, *The Critical Theory of Lord Kames*, in *Smith College Studies in Modern Languages*, XXII (1941), 82.

12. *Lectures in Rhetoric and Belles Lettres*, Lecture XVIII. Because of the large number of editions and printings of this work, some in one and some in two volumes, with varying pagination, and because the individual lectures are all comparatively short, reference will be made throughout this study to the lecture number, which will be the same in all editions, rather than to page

For him both in their highest forms arise from heightened imagination or from inflamed passion and have essentially the same purpose—persuasion:

The ultimate end of all poetry, indeed of every composition, should be to make some useful impression on the mind. This useful impression is most commonly made in poetry by indirect methods; as by fable, by narration, by representation of character. . . . The poet must instruct; but he must study, at the same time, to enliven his instructions by the introduction of such figures and such circumstances, as may amuse the imagination, may conceal the dryness of his subject, and embellish it with poetical painting.[13]

He felt that the purpose of poetry differs from that of oratory mainly in degree or in the means employed.

The kinship of the two modes appears again in the concept of taste, which was of central importance to his esthetics. To him taste was "the power of receiving pleasure from the beauties of nature and art"; it was a critical ability which could most easily be acquired by a study of rhetoric, the word "rhetoric" becoming for him an omnibus term meaning the entire field of language and literature. Thus in his long discussion of taste, oratory and poetry are treated as two slightly different aspects of the same thing. When pushed to distinguish poetry from other discourse, Blair fell back like many of his contemporaries on safe ground. Poetry is "the language of passion, or enlivened imagination, formed most commonly into regular numbers,"[14] and elsewhere the poetic style differs from that of prose "not in point of numbers only, but in the very words themselves." Poetry is most fully to be distinguished from prose (including oratory) by its meter, rime, and poetic diction. Of deeper and more philosophic distinctions he had nothing to say; he thought of such distinctions as "the minutiae of criticism, concerning which frivolous writers are always disposed to squabble; but which deserve not any particular discussion."[15]

---

number. This procedure will be followed with respect to Kames *Elements* for similar reasons.

13. *Lectures,* XL.   14. *Ibid.,* XXXVIII.

15. *Ibid.* Blair repeatedly stated that passion and enlivened imagination are present in the higher forms of oratory just as much as in poetry. But I find nothing in his remarks to suggest that he thought poetic diction appropriate to oratory. It seems justifiable in view of this omission to suppose that he thought of poetic diction as appropriate only to verse.

George Campbell went much further than Blair and made an explicit identification of rhetoric and poetic. In the first chapter of *The Philosophy of Rhetoric* he made the startling claim that

Poetry, indeed, is properly no other than a particular mode or form of certain branches of oratory. . . . The direct end of the former, whether to delight the fancy, as in epic, or to move the passions, as in tragedy, is avowedly in part the aim, and sometimes the immediate and proposed aim, of the orator. The same medium, language, is made use of, the same general rules of composition, in narration, description, argumentation, are observed; and the same tropes and figures, either for beautifying or for invigorating the diction are employed by both. In regard to versification, it is more to be considered as an appendage than as a constituent of poetry. In this lies what may be called the more mechanical part of the poet's work, being at most but a sort of garnishing, and by far too unessential to give a designation to the kind. This particularity in form, to adopt an expression of the naturalists, constitutes only a variety, and not a different species.

Campbell was obviously thinking in terms at once more basic and more inclusive than Blair. The versification on which Blair grounded his distinction Campbell disallowed completely, but the result was an even more explicit identification of the two through the subsuming of poetry under rhetoric.[16] To him epic was oratory appealing to the imagination; tragedy was oratory appealing to the passions.[17] Because for him the distinction between the two modes of discourse had broken down, he saw nothing to hinder his transferring the whole poetic function and method over into rhetoric. He represents the most extreme position, but the fact that no one rose to denounce him as a heretic shows that he cannot have been far out of touch with the temper of his time. Far from being denounced in America, his book was adopted by a number of colleges as a textbook to supplement Blair.[18]

---

16. Cf. Gordon MacKenzie's remark to this effect in *Critical Responsiveness: A Study of the Psychological Current in Later Eighteenth-Century Criticism,* University of California Publications in English, No. 20 (Berkeley, 1949), p. 61.

17. Campbell, p. 25.

18. According to Guthrie (pp. 88-89), Campbell's *The Philosophy of Rhetoric* was known in America soon after its publication in 1776, but it did not become widely popular until after 1820. After this date it began to rival Blair somewhat as a college textbook, though even at this time it was often used not as a replacement but as a supplement to Blair.

To these lines of rhetorical influence converging from the Augustan poets and from the literary and rhetorical theorists must be added another—the influence of such ancient poets as Horace. There are signs of his influence everywhere. In the poetry sections of the magazines appear dozens of translations or imitations of his works; the critics in these same periodicals mention his name or quote his critical precepts innumerable times, and always with deference. *The Ars Poetica* as well as the Odes and Epistles was a standard part of the college curriculum, and where rhetoric did not come in the front door with Horace himself, it came in the back door through his influence on the English Augustans. Perhaps of equal importance with any first-hand American acquaintance with his works was the fact that his critical precepts were spread in America through the theory and practice of the English neoclassic poets and critics. Caroline Goad has shown in her study of Horace's influence on eighteenth-century English literature that in the work of those poets and critics

Horace was the most frequently quoted and deferred to of any classic author—deferred to even more generally than Virgil with his . . . purer poetic genius, and more often than the much-quoted Cicero. . . . [There was] a noticeable tendency to use the Satires and Epistles more than the Odes, and, where the Odes were used, to select those parts that would have some utilitarian value.[19]

His influence, she found, was especially strong in providing rules for the literary artist. And another scholar claims that Dryden's criticism is so permeated with Horace that if the *Ars Poetica* should by chance be lost, it could be largely reconstructed from Dryden's references to it,[20] and that to trace Dryden's influence on subsequent literature is, to a large extent, to trace the influence of Horace.[21] The significance of this strong influence of Horace can more readily be appreciated when Baldwin's statement is recalled: that in Horace's circle the distinction between rhetoric and poetic as two movements, two ways of composing, seems to have been inactive, and that thus under the Empire grammarians, rhetoricians, philoso-

19. *Horace in the English Literature of the Eighteenth Century*, in *Yale Studies in English*, LVIII (New Haven, 1918), p. 7.
20. Amanda M. Ellis, "Horace's Influence on Dryden," *Philological Quarterly*, IV (1925), 42.
21. *Ibid.*, p. 59.

phers, and poets seemed to converge toward a poetic strongly tinged with rhetoric.[22]

American critics were generally unconcerned about the relationship of rhetoric and poetic. There were a few notable exceptions, particularly John Witherspoon who made clear distinctions between the two modes in terms of maker, purpose, address, and method— though not in any connected discussion, but in remarks scattered here and there throughout the *Lectures*.[23]

In 1805 an anonymous contributor to the *Monthly Anthology* made the following distinction between the two modes:

Poetry is the frolick of invention, the dame of words, and the harmony of sounds. Oratory consists in a judicious disposition of arguments: a happy selection of terms, and in a pleasing elocution. The object of poetry is to delight, that of oratory is to persuade. Poetry is truth, but it is truth in her gayest and loveliest robes, and wit, flattery, hyperbole, and fable are marshalled in her train. Oratory has a graver and more majestic port, and gains by slow advances and perseverance what the poet takes by the suddenness of his inspiration and by surprise. Poetry requires genius; eloquence is within the reach of talent.[24]

Such systematic statements as this are rare during this period, and what is more important, they seem to have exerted no influence on poetic practice. Most poets and critics would no doubt have admitted, if asked point-blank, that there were great differences between poetry and rhetoric, but they did not elect to discuss the differences. They were more inclined to assume, as Blair did, that there was no need for being "very precise about the boundaries as long as the nature of each is understood." But there are many signs that the two were closely associated in their minds. Throughout the criticism, in any discussion of literary art in general, or in any listing of the fine arts, poetry is almost invariably linked with

22. Charles S. Baldwin, *Ancient Rhetoric and Poetic* (New York, 1924), pp. 244-246.

23. John Witherspoon, *Lectures on Moral Philosophy and Rhetoric* (Woodward's 3rd ed., Philadelphia, 1810), pp. 185-187; see also pp. 152 and 202.

24. *Monthly Anthology and Boston Review*, II (1805), 636-637. The article "Poetry" in the *Encyclopedia or Dictionary of Arts, Sciences and Miscellaneous Literature* (Philadelphia, 1790) distinguished between the two modes with considerable acumen, and a discussion of poetry in George Gregory's *Dictionary of Arts and Sciences* (Charleston, 1815-1816), which apparently owed much to the more comprehensive *Encyclopedia,* made a distinction with similar philosophic detachment.

37

oratory, or "eloquence" as current usage had it. Even Witherspoon associates them thus in his *Lectures,* and this is only one of the respects in which his book resembled Blair's. Although "eloquence" primarily meant oratory to Witherspoon, it did not exclude poetry; his treatise discusses not only the art of composing and delivering a speech, but devotes a great deal of space to the nature and kinds of poetry. His chief emphasis throughout the book is on *elocutio* or style, the element of discourse in which the two modes have always had the most in common.

According to most American critics, the chief differentia between poetry and prose (including oratory) was the same one Blair had stressed—verse, or "number." A long article in *The Lady's Magazine and Repository of Useful Information* (1792) found that poetry and oratory have much in common, including "elevation of thought, sublimity of sentiment, boldness of figure, grandeur of description, or embellishment of imagination."[25] The main conclusion of the article is that poetry and prose "like two colors easily distinguishable in their pure, unmixed state, melt into one another by almost imperceptible shades till the distinction is entirely lost."[26] Poetry is most readily to be distinguished from prose by means of its "regular numbers."

Rime, meter, and poetic diction were commonly felt to be enough by themselves to render any discourse poetic. Starting with the assumption that "there is such a charm in metre and poetical language that the weakest of matter is . . . often graced in rhyme,"[27] poetasters of this time versified speeches, histories, the Psalms of David and other passages of scripture, and even such things as geography texts for school children.[28] Apparently, no matter was thought to be so "weak" as to be unfit for the graces of rime and meter. Jonathan Sewall put Washington's *Farewell Address* into verse because, he said, "verse commonly makes a deeper impression

25. These bear close resemblance to Longinus' listing of the chief elements of the sublime. See *Longinus on the Sublime,* trans. by W. Rhys Roberts (Cambridge, 1907), Chapter VIII.

26. *The Lady's Magazine,* I (1792), 151-159.

27. Charles Prentiss, *A Collection of Fugitive Essays in Prose and Verse* (Leominster, Mass., 1797), p. 24.

28. See for example Chapman Whitcomb, *Geography Epitomized. A short but Comprehensive Description of the Terraqueous Globe, in Verse* . . . (Leominster, Mass., 1796?); or Victorianus Clark, *A Rhyming Geography, or, A Poetic Description of the United States of America* (Hartford, 1819).

and is more easily retained in the memory than prose."[29] At the same time he recognized that many subjects in the address were "improper for poetry."

These versifiers derived sanction from Virgil's *Georgics*, from the didactic works of Pope, and from the precedent set by such popular poems as Erasmus Darwin's "The Botanic Garden" (1789). The intention of such didactic verse was worthy enough—to improve upon prose and to render worth-while subjects more delightful. But the prose which they intended to improve upon lost its integrity as prose, and the verse which they produced was debased by being harnessed to prosaic materials and purposes.

Considering the large number of such poems, it is no wonder that many persons felt that poetry in both England and America was on the decline.[30] Some echoed the primitivistic idea of Kames and Blair that poetry flourishes best in the early ages of a civilization, that it later achieves elegance, and finally declines into *"nugae canorae,* or the tinkling of mere versifiers."[31] They felt America to be in a strange position: it was in its early age of development, and yet it could produce no Homer because sophisticated and decadent models of poetry from England had been inflicted upon its poetry from without. They recognized that the performance of contemporary poets in no way measured up to that of the giants of the past, and insisted upon the sanctity of rime, meter, and poetic diction as the last distinguishing marks of a poetry which, except for these, would be swallowed up in the sea of oratory and other forms of prose.[32]

Thus all roads through poetic practice and precept lead to the conclusion that few persons saw any reason to make clear distinctions between rhetoric and poetic discourse. Rhetoric dominated literary theory partly because every major source from which theory was drawn was either directly or indirectly rhetorical.

29. *A Versification of President Washington's Excellent Farewell Address* . . . (Portsmouth, N. H. 1798), Preface. Reprinted in *The Magazine of History with Notes and Queries,* extra no. 108, vol. 27, no. 2 (Tarrytown, N. Y., n.d.), pp. 31-71.
30. For example, see *Port Folio*, V (1805), 193.
31. *Monthly Anthology*, I (1804), 507.
32. See *The Lady's Magazine*, I (1792), 158.

4. DIDACTICISM

Few American poets of the early national period felt the innate urge which seems to have motivated Spenser or Milton or other great poets. No American poet spoke like Pope of "lisping in numbers, *for the numbers came*"; none was moved like Chatterton by an urge to write poetry so strong that he was willing to starve to satisfy it; none spoke like Shelley and Wordsworth of being "dedicated spirits." Such a motive for writing poetry no American of this period felt, with the exception of Freneau and Trumbull, and in neither of these men was it strong enough to maintain itself for long against the hostile forces in the American environment. This may be one way of saying that American poets lacked poetic genius, but it serves better than anything else to explain why so much of the poetry lacks inner spirit or force, why so much of it seems hollow or contrived, rationalistically rather than imaginatively conceived.

Both Barlow and Dwight, whose epics constitute the most ambitious poetic works of the period, were moved mainly by rationalistic, unduly self-conscious motives. A great epic seemed to them essential to establish the dignity of America in the arts, and they set about with determination to produce it; but their attention was centered not so much on the poem as on the greatness of America. Another of the Connecticut Wits, David Humphreys, whose poems were popular in his own day, was driven to write many of them by the practical desire of gaining advancement. Leon Howard says of Humphreys that "his thoughts turned productively to literature whenever he was threatened with the loss of a job or needed to attract attention in order to gain preferment."[1] This utilitarian motive was certainly one of the reasons why Humphreys' poems are among the most rhetorical of those produced in this age of rhetorical poetry.

The literary criticism insisted upon inspiration and "original genius" in poetry, but the wide gap between theory and practice in eighteenth-century England was also noticeable in America. In a poem called *The Powers of Genius* (1795), John Blair Linn wrote that

1. *The Connecticut Wits* (Chicago, 1943), pp. 36-37.

40

> The poet often gains a madman's name
> When first he kindles with the muse's flame,
> When wild and startling he appears in pain
> And shows a moon-struck phrenzy of the brain.[2]

He found that in too much poetry of this time

> Taste is confined to rules, it moves in chains;
> Genius those fetters and those rules disdains.[3]

This is straight orthodoxy in theory, an idea with which all his contemporaries would have agreed. John Blair Linn himself, however, did not notice, nor did any of his contemporaries call the fact to his attention, that the very verse he uses to insist upon the primary place of genius is utterly conventional, fettered by the very rules against which it speaks.

Genius may have been considered essential to the poetic function, but no one in America was deterred by such a theoretical belief from writing verse. Some versifiers who were aware of their deficiencies went on writing poetry because they considered it a patriotic and moral duty. Richard Snowden's remarks, in the preface to his *Columbiad* (1795), go beyond the conventional modesty of prefaces to an honest admission of his meager abilities as a poet. He explains that he is writing the poem because no one else has written a suitable poem on the American Revolution, and he hopes that his effort will stimulate "someone more favoured of the muses who will undertake the arduous task."[4]

Few poets, mediocre or not, care to admit a lack of genius, and there are understandably few statements by American poets which proclaim the fact as publicly as does Snowden. There is an unusual sobriety and lack of humor in the American view of poetry. Notable exceptions may be found in the Connecticut Wits in their more satiric or playful moods, but even they ordinarily looked upon poetry as a solemn business, and this general gravity permitted excesses which a better perspective would not have allowed. Even when they did recognize the mediocrity of their best attempts, they were unwilling to proclaim the fact because they feared that such

---

2. *The Powers of Genius, a Poem in Three Parts* (2nd ed., Philadelphia, 1802) p. 29.   3. *Ibid.*, p. 37.

4. *The Columbiad, or, a Poem on the American War in Thirteen Cantos* (Philadelphia, 1795), Preface. Not to be confused with Barlow's better known *Columbiad* published in 1807.

an admission would diminish the greatness of Amercia and increase the greatness of England. They believed so sincerely that under the blessings of a free government all the faculties of man, including his poetic abilities, would by nature develop to a higher perfection than under the corruption and oppression of the monarchies of Europe, and they were so anxious to convince the rest of the world of this, that they would do nothing to prejudice the idea. Unfortunately, as noble as this determination was, it could not raise the quality of their poetry. Their theories of greatness in poetry would not allow them to regard with seriousness the lighter forms of verse—satire, mock-heroic, burlesque, minor lyric—in which they sometimes did equal their contemporaries in England, and they continued in spite of their limitations to write poetry in the grand manner, determined to raise the reputation of their country in the eyes of the world.

This statement agrees with Herbert W. Schneider's observation that the actions of American men of affairs during this period were consciously shaped by the feeling that they were acting under the scrutiny of the whole world. "The conspicuous fact about American life then," he says, "was that not only were the eyes and hopes of the world centered on America, but also American men of affairs themselves were genuinely concerned with the wider, if not the universal implications of their interests and deeds. They had, indeed, a 'decent respect of the opinions of mankind. . . . ' Never was history made more consciously and conscientiously."[5] It was because of the poets' strong sense of mission, because the ends they hoped to achieve were to them so noble and so compelling, that they continued to write poetry, lack of genius and other limitations notwithstanding. Their strong desire to achieve worthy ends seems commonly to have served in place of deep poetic impulse. This leads to an inquiry into those ends for which they labored with such diligence and genuine disregard of self.

Neglecting light verse for the moment, the love-laments, the clever epigrams, the rimed conundrums and puzzles, the conventional eclogues, and the other *vers de société*, and considering only poems on serious subjects, we find that most American poetry of this period was written for one or more of the following purposes: (1) to glorify America, (2) to glorify democractic or republican principles of government and society, (3) to lead men to virtue by

5. *A History of American Philosophy* (New York, 1946), pp. 35-36.

inculcating moral truth. All three of these ends, it can be seen at once, are more readily served by rhetorical than by poetic techniques. This estimate of purpose is based on the poetry itself; the emphasis in the critical writings is somewhat different. The critical statements of purpose commonly pivot around Horace's maxim that poets either profit or please, or profit and please, at the same time; and the evidence points to a nearly unanimous insistence that poetry should inculcate moral truth. That poetry should please as well as instruct was not denied, but this was considered to be its lesser function or a function preliminary to the other. Some persons, like Witherspoon, allowed the lesser forms of poetry to have a predominantly pleasurable function, but most critics did not yield even this much and insisted that even comedy and satire should "correct whilst they divert us and wage implacable war with vice and folly."[6]

Patriotism was often closely associated with morality, and to preach democracy was sometimes considered much the same as preaching morality. This mixture shows plainy in Barlow who wanted to "make patriot views and moral views the same."[7] In reply to the statement of the Bishop of Blois that the *Columbiad* was detrimental to religion, Barlow made this assertion:

I believe, and you have compelled me on this occasion to express my belief, that the Columbiad, taken in all its parts of text and notes and preface, is more favorable to sound and rigorous morals, more friendly to virtue, more clear and unequivocal in pointing out the road to national dignity and individual happiness, more energetic in its denunciations of tyranny and oppression in every shape, injustice and wickedness in all their forms, and consequently more consonant to what you acknowledge to be the spirit of the gospel than all the writings of all that list of Christian authors of the three last ages whom you have cited as the glory of Christendom. . . . I judge not my poem as a work of genius. . . . But I *know* it is a moral work; I *can* judge and *dare* pronounce upon its tendency, its beneficial effect upon every candid mind.[8]

The blend of morality with democratic principles is seen most

6. *The Boston Magazine,* I (1783), 110.
7. *The Conspiracy of Kings* (London, 1792), reprinted in V. L. Parrington, ed., *The Connecticut Wits,* p. 348.
8. Letter to Henri Grégoire, Bishop of Blois, quoted in W. B. Otis, *American Verse, 1625-1807* (New York, 1909), pp. 168-169.

plainly in the preface to the *Columbiad* where he says that the object of the poem is

to inculcate the love of rational liberty, and to discountenance the deleterious passions for violence and war; to show that on the basis of the republican principle all good morals, as well as good government and hopes of permanent peace must be founded. . . . My object is altogether of a moral and political nature. I wish to encourage and strengthen, in the rising generation a sense of the importance of republican institutions; as being the great foundation of public and private happiness, the necessary element of future and permanent meliorations in the conditions of human nature.

Richard Beresford in 1793 pointed out that

poetry in other times and governments, wherein the rights of man were unknown or trampled on, having sometimes taken a wrong direction, misled and hurt mankind. The morals of the two great epic poems of antiquity are bad in essentials, and took their complexions from the licentious manners of the ages in which they were composed.[9]

Proper morality and political principles in poetry were insisted upon because these men believed that "the advantage of liberty . . . can be secured so well by nothing as by the aids of literature."[10] They felt it their duty to substitute Christian principles of morality and democratic principles of government for the barbarous morality and tyrannous political philosophies contained in the epics of Homer and Virgil. Beresford's general thesis was that since in a republic the whole function and welfare of the state depends upon the virtue of individual citizens, poetry and all other forms of literature should be encouraged as a means of propagating virtue. "Virtue," he said, "must not only be known but recommended; and the distinction between the charms of truth attired in homely vestments, or graced in all the ornaments of rhetoric and poetry, fails not to strike the eye of an ordinary beholder. . . ."[11] Timothy Dwight, too, remarked in the introduction to *Greenfield Hill* (1794) that poetry "will be read by many persons who would scarcely look at a logical discussion, and by most readers it will be more deeply felt and more lastingly remembered."

9. *A Plea for Literature: More Especially the Literature of Free States* (Charleston, 1793), p. 28.
10. *Ibid.*, p. 72. 11. *Ibid.*, p. 25.

This insistence on morality and constructive political views in poetry is understandable in men who felt the eyes of the world upon them. Nor should it be overlooked that many of them, in spite of their acquaintance with rationalistic philosophers of the enlightenment, were descendants of the Puritans and were still actively professing their inherited Calvinism. Lewis Leary said of John Blair Linn, "We can emphasize his confusion of poetry with religion, which made the voice of the poet the distillation of the voice of God, and the end of the poetry uncompromisingly moral."[12] This identification of religion with poetry is apparent in Timothy Dwight, especially in such places as the fifth and sixth part of *Greenfield Hill,* where his declared purpose was "to excite [his parishioners'] attention to the truths and duties of religion" and "to promote in them just sentiments and useful conduct for the present life."[13] In 1789 Charles Brockden Brown remarked that "the enthusiasm of religion is little different from that of poetry and these are with great difficulty distinguished from a sublime and rational philosophy. . . . The effects of their several propensities are exactly similar."[14] John Quincy Adams stated quite bluntly that moral principle "should be the alpha and omega of all human composition, poetry, or prose, scientific or literary, written or spoken."[15] Dryden, Pope, Cowper, and the other British poets highly regarded by Americans were praised above all for their moral teaching. A reviewer wrote, "In the *Task* of Cowper there is no licentiousness of description. All is grave and majestic, and moral. A vein of religious thinking pervades every page, and he discourses in a strain of the most finished poetry on the insufficiency of vanity of human pursuits."[16] Barlow's reputation among his countrymen rested eventually not on his ability as a poet, but on the worthiness of his aims.

12. "John Blair Linn, 1775-1805," *William and Mary Quarterly,* 3rd series, IV (1947), 176.

13. *Greenfield Hill* (New York, 1794), Introduction.

14. *The Rhapsodist and Other Uncollected Writings,* ed. Harry R. Warfel, in *Scholars Facsimiles and Reprints* (New York, 1943), p. 8.

15. *Memoirs,* ed. C. F. Adams (Philadelphia, 1874-1877), XI, 372. Other statements that poetry should have primarily a moral and persuasive purpose appear in: *Port Folio,* IV (1804), 166, 377, 398; V (1805), 171; new [3rd] series, IV (1810), 453; *Baltimore Repertory,* I (1811), 1-3; *The American Magazine,* I (1788), 471; *Massachusetts Magazine,* IV (1792), 4-5; V (1799), 227; *Monthly Anthology and Boston Review,* II (1805), 168, 211; IV (1807), 135, 466-469; *Universal Asylum and Columbian Magazine,* VI (1791), 318.

16. *Monthly Magazine and American Review,* III (1800), 226.

They forgave his lack of the one because of their approval of the other. Charles Jared Ingersoll, wrote in 1810,

The good of mankind, much more than their pleasure, seems to have been the end of his work. . . . As a moral vision broadly based in historical truth, with a due admixture of fiction and poetic machinery, constructed of interesting incidents, intersected with agreeable episodes, and conducted to an instructive catastrophe, the Columbiad will always be admired. If the words could be transposed so as to remove every vestige of versification without impairing the sense and beauty of this composition, it would still be read, and read with pleasure, as a chaste, moral and elegant performance. But its charms lie more in the moral of the design and force of the argument than in the poetic charm of the execution.[17]

This strong insistence on the moral function of poetry Americans could have found nearly everywhere present in English neoclassic theory and practice from Ben Jonson to Charles Churchill. Nor was there any lessening in emphasis on morality with the adoption of the new ideas of taste and the sublime. The Scottish rhetoricians, who were chiefly responsible for bringing these new ideas to America, had imbibed deeply of Shaftesbury's doctrines which insisted on the close connection between esthetic good taste and moral goodness. One of Blair's chief arguments for studying rhetoric went like this: the study of rhetoric results in a sharpened critical sense; this leads to a refined taste; and this in turn leads to moral conduct.[18] The cultivation of taste tends to bring out all that is good in a man, and to weaken or suppress all that is evil. He sums up its effect: "I will not go so far as to say that improvement of taste and virtue is the same; or they may always be expected to co-exist in an equal degree. . . . At the same time, this cannot but be admitted, that the exercise of taste is, in its native tendency, moral and purifying."[19] There are many echoes of this Shaftesburyan idea in American critical statements, for example the following from Dennie's *Port Folio:* "An intimate acquaintance with the good poets

17. *Inchiquin; the Jesuit's Letters* (New York, 1810), p. 81. Samuel Kettell expressed the same opinion in 1829, in his anthology of American verse: "The moral scope of the work, in spite of its miscarriage as an epic, will recommend it to our regard as the earnest endeavor of a sincere philanthropist to further the progress of the human race in their advances to political and moral perfection." *Specimens of American Poetry* (Boston, 1829), II, 13.
18. *Lectures,* Introduction.
19. *Ibid.,* I.

will enable us to detect the faults of the bad; and let it be remembered that this is no trifling accomplishment if it be true that a good taste in literature generally leads to a correct taste in politics, morals, and religion."[20] One statement in the *Monthly Anthology* claimed that the cultivated taste resulting from a close acquaintance with literature can enhance a man's religious potential.[21]

Moral suasion was not the only function allowed to poetry, but coupled as it frequently was with the glorification of America and of republican principles, it appears to have been the most important one. It is true that in the periodicals there were hundreds of little narrative pieces, conventional eclogues, love laments, and humorous or lightly satirical poems, which had as their chief purpose to divert or amuse; but many even of these had some moral cast.

Public insistence on the moral element in art ran so strong in Rhode Island during the early years of the Revolution that Shakespeare's *Othello* could be performed only by being advertised as "*Moral Dialogues in Five Parts,* Depicting the Effects of Jealousy, and Other Bad Passions, and proving that happiness can only spring from the pursuit of virtue." This handbill went on to promise that "various other dialogues [i.e. plays by Shakespeare] . . . all adapted to the improvement of the mind and manners would be delivered. Commencement at 7, conclusion at half past 10, in order that every spectator may go home at a sober hour and reflect upon what he has seen before he retires to rest."[22] If Shakespeare had to be soaked in so thick a molasses of moral sentiment to be made palatable, it should not be surprising that American authors felt moved to be edifying.

20. IV (1804), 398.
21. IV (1807), 467.
22. John Bernard, *Retrospections of America, 1797-1811* (New York, 1887), pp. 270-271.

5. PROPAGANDA AND DECLAMATION

Most poetry of the early republic, vigorous as it was, makes dull reading today. We can hear in it the heightened voice of the poet, speaking urgently or flamboyantly, but his words fall to the ground before they reach our ears; they are only for that other audience, now dead. We sense that the poet is thinking only of them and is speaking of their crisis or their triumph, which is not ours. We cannot feel moved to resist marauding Hessians, or to hate Tories, or to join the armies of Washington as he marches toward Yorktown. The urgency which gave this poetry its life is gone, and if we can look at it with the same interest and curiosity as we look at other parts of the historical record, we cannot be much moved by it. This poetry is so little ours because it belongs too much to its own time—which is one way of saying that it lacks the universalized audience and subject matter which are typical of the best poetry, and shows the more narrow awareness of audience and occasion which are typical of rhetoric.

Most of the serious verse of this time can be described as either *partisan* or *epideictic*. Partisan poems are simply versified propaganda, designed to move a particular group of men to some desired action, to persuade them to believe in one cause or to reject another. Such poems typically show a strong awareness of a definite audience and occasion, and may have, in addition to a dominant purpose to persuade, some admixture of praise or blame. In poems of this kind there may be considerable heat of emotion, but the language tends to be direct and fairly simple. Except for style, similar elements are present in epideictic poems, but they are combined in different proportion. The term "epideictic" itself, as borrowed from classical rhetoric, implies definite occasion and audience and a dominant purpose of praise or blame, along with highly ornamented, extravagant style. Epideictic poems are usually written "to order" to celebrate a wedding, or the opening of a new theater, or a victory in war, to lament the passing of some great man, or to heap abuse upon the head of some public villain.

Poems of both types are occasional in the sense that they are attached to contemporary military, political, social, or religious events. Freneau furnishes a good example; his writing career spans the whole forty-year period under consideration in this study and his poems consistently reflect contemporary events. The early revolutionary years are represented by such poems as "General Gage's Soliloquy" (1775), "On a Hessian Debarkation" (1776); the later Revolution by "On the Memorable Victory of Paul Jones" (1781), and by his many poems directed against the Tory printer, James Rivington. The most stirring event of the nineties is represented by such poems as "On the Prospect of a Revolution in France" (1790), "On the Fourteenth of July" (1792), "On the Demolition of the French Monarchy" (1792). One of the founding fathers is mourned in "On the Death of Dr. Benjamin Franklin" (1790), and ten years later another is lamented in "Stanzas upon the Memory of General Washington" (1800). A threatened war is reflected in "On the War Projected with the Republic of France" (1797). The Alien and Sedition Acts are commented upon in "Stanzas to an Alien" (1799). Jefferson's retirement from the presidency is noted in "Lines Addressed to Mr. Jefferson" (1809), and many poems record events connected with the War of 1812. Freneau's concern with contemporary events and with democratic principles began with the opening of his poetic career in 1768 and did not end till his death in 1832.

The same occasional note pervades the poetry of all the other chief poets of the period, though none was as prolific as Freneau. Timothy Dwight wrote such poems as "Address of the Genius of Columbus: To the Members of the Continental Congress" (1788?); Trumbull vigorously protested the British blockade of Boston harbor in 1775 in a poem entitled "An Elegy on the Times"; Humphreys in "A Poem on the Happiness of America" (1785) painted the horrors experienced by American seamen imprisoned as slaves by the Algerian pirates. Robert Treat Paine's poems not only reflect political or social events, but most of them were written to order for various ceremonial occasions in and around Boston. Their titles tell the story accurately enough: "Prize Prologue . . . spoken at the opening of the first theatre in Boston, January 1794"; "Ode, written for and sung at the Anniversary of the Massachusetts Association for improving the Breed of Horses, October 21, 1811." Many poems were written for occasions of even more local or personal importance, such as Humphreys' sonnet "Addressed to my Friends at Yale College, on my Leaving them to Join the Army."

49

Few poets can avoid giving some reflection of their own time and place in their poetry, and it is illegitimate to expect that they should. But the better poets are able to endow even parochial materials with larger significance—something which happens relatively seldom in American verse of the early national period. It is difficult to imagine another large body of verse which so universally begins and ends in the occasions which prompted it.

As one might expect of poetry closely attached to occasion and chiefly governed by purposes of persuasion, praise, or blame, most of it also narrowed its appeal to specific audiences. Nearly all of it faces toward an audience of Americans, or "Columbians." Even the epics, those poems most intended by their authors to be for all mankind and for all time, show that they are directed chiefly to Americans and are concerned largely with contemporary affairs. Barlow devoted four whole books of the *Columbiad* to events in the American Revolution, and Timothy Dwight's *Conquest of Canaan,* though it offends least in this respect among epic poems of the time, indulges in thinly-veiled allegory in which the struggles of Joshua in conquering the land of Canaan are supposed to suggest the struggles of Washington in the Revolution.

Frequently, while writing for their American audience, these poets struck out against some other audience, usually eschewing the rapier of wit for the meat axe of scurrilous personal abuse, as in these remarks directed by Freneau to Lord Cornwallis:

> Quick, let the halter end thee or the knife;
> So may destruction rush with speedy wing,
> Low as yourself, to drag your cruel king;
> His head torn off, his hands, his feet, and all,
> Deep in the dust may Dagon's image fall;
> His stump alone escape the vengeful steel,
> Sav'd but to grace the gibbet or the wheel.[1]

Many poems were addressed to narrower audiences than Americans in general, especially after the Revolution when the unity inspired by effort against a common foe began to disintegrate and factions of many kinds began to take form. One of the most widespread divisions in American society was that between "democrat" and "aristocrat," a division which later crystallized in the Repub-

1. *The Poems of Philip Freneau,* ed. F. L. Pattee (Princeton, 1902-1907), II, 100.

lican and Federalist parties. Of the poets supporting the cause of democracy, Freneau was the most eloquent and prolific. In 1792 he made quite clear that his first book of verse (1785) had been

> Hostile to garter, ribbon, crown, and star;
> Still on the people's, still on Freedom's side,
> With full determin'd aim, to baffle every claim
> Of well-born wights, that aim'd to mount and ride.[2]

Another poet who became a vigorous champion of democracy was Joel Barlow. His virile "Conspiracy of Kings" (1792) bore the subtitle "A Poem Addressed to the Inhabitants of Europe from another Quarter of the Globe"—and by "inhabitants" Barlow meant the common people of Europe. That his poem was slanted to an audience of democrats can be seen from the way he bloodied the crowned heads of Europe and what he called their paid lackeys, the ecclesiastics of the established churches. Other poets stoutly defended the aristocratic position, among them Dwight, Trumbull, Humphreys, Alsop, and Robert Treat Paine, and slanted their poems toward a different segment of society.[3]

In the 1790's party and class views were often expressed in terms of praise or dispraise of France, with Freneau the democrat, as might be expected, consistently praising France and the Revolution, though many voices were raised in protest after the Reign of Terror and after the French armies began their march of conquest over Europe.[4] Still another type of special audience is revealed in Timothy Dwight's *Triumph of Infidelity* (1788) which seems to have been written for Protestants who espoused the same orthodox brand of Calvinism as Dwight himself. Nearly every other important religious group in the Western world, and some in the Eastern, came in for severe abuse, though he concentrated his fire on deists, atheists, Roman Catholics, and Unitarians.

But there is no need here to fingerprint each separate variation of audience and occasion; a simple numerical count can show how much of this poetry is either partisan or epideictic. Of the 368 poems in Pattee's edition of Freneau's poetry, all but 83 are of these two types. David Humphreys' principal poems are all epideictic,

2. *Poems*, III, 78-79.
3. Trumbull's *McFingal*, for example, looks *away* from the lower classes and *toward* the Whig aristocracy.
4. See for example Robert Treat Paine, *The Works in Prose and Verse* (Boston, 1812), p. 250.

as are the greater number of Francis Hopkinson's poems, which are divided by his biographer into three groups: "(1) occasional lyrics, elegies, birthday pieces, complimentary addresses and college exercises; (2) 'political ballads,' written to check the despondency and arouse the fighting spirit of his countrymen during the Revolution; (3) songs for which he composed music."[5] In the *Works* of Robert Treat Paine, out of 87 separate poems, at least 66 are clearly epideictic and many others have some epideictic cast. The poems on which his rather considerable contemporary fame rested—and the poems for which he is chiefly recalled today—are all epideictic pieces: "The Ruling Passion, an occasional poem, written by the appointment of the Phi Beta Kappa, and spoken, on their anniversary, in the chapel of the university, Cambridge, July 20, 1797," "The Invention of Letters: a Poem, written at the request of the president of Harvard University; and delivered in Cambridge, on the day of annual commencement, July 15, 1795." Most of Trumbull's poems fall into these two categories, as do the lesser poems of Barlow and Dwight. And even in the periodicals, poems of these types are most numerous. In the *Universal Asylum and Columbian Magazine* out of some 237 poems published in the poet's corner during the years 1790-1792, 95 or nearly half were partisan or epideictic pieces. The percentage was even higher in the second volume of the *Monthly Magazine and American Review* (1800) in which, out of 34 poems published in the poetry section, 21 were odes with a decided epideictic cast. And besides these, three other odes on the death of Washington were printed or reviewed in other sections.[6]

5. George Hastings, *The Life and Works of Francis Hopkinson* (Chicago, 1926), p. 466. A contemporary critic wrote concerning the effect of Hopkinson's political verse: "the various causes which contributed to the establishment of the independence and federal government of the United States will not be fully traced, unless much is ascribed to the irresistible influence of the ridicule which he poured forth, from time to time, upon the enemies of those great political events." *Massachusetts Magazine*, III (1791), 751.

6. The findings of C. W. Coles in his study of literary nationalism during the last quarter of the eighteenth century are of interest: "During the Revolution and the Period of Confederation [1775-1788], three out of every ten poems which were printed in magazines contained some type of patriotic exploitation; in the 1790 decade the proportion increased. These percentages reveal a considerable preoccupation with native materials motivated by patriotic and nationalistic impulses." "The Growth of Nationalism in American Literature 1775-1800" (unpublished dissertation, George Washington University, 1948), p. 317. His figures are lower than those cited above since he was counting

So strong was the declamatory note that it invaded many poems not intended to be primarily epideictic. Timothy Dwight undoubtedly thought of *Greenfield Hill* (1794) as a topographical poem after the model of Denham's "Cooper's Hill," but nothing in Denham licensed the full-throated extravagance of Dwight's panegyric to New England (requiring more than half of Part I) or the extended encomium to clergymen which he uses as a thumping peroration. Nor was Dwight alone; the *Columbiad* of his fellow Connecticut Wit, Barlow, was often a tissue of epideictic pieces, as witness the following portion of the Argument to Book VIII: "Hymn to Peace. Eulogy on the heroes slain in the war; address to the patriots who have survived the conflict, exhorting them to preserve the liberty they have established. . . . Atlas, the guardian Genius of Africa, denounces to Hesper the crimes of his people in the slavery of the African. . . ."

Not infrequently a poet pulled down all the barriers but verse itself between oration and poem and unabashedly labeled his "poem" an oration in verse. The extreme degree of influence from specific audience and occasion can be seen in Hopkinson's poem entitled, "An Oration which Might Have Been Delivered to the Students in Anatomy on the Late Rupture Between the Two Schools in Philadelphia" (1789); or in Trumbull's "Funeral Oration"; or in Robert Treat Paine's "Dedicatory Address; Spoken by Mr. Hodgkinson, October 29, 1798, at the Opening of the New Federal Theatre, in Boston." Twitch aside at any point the mantle of verse laid over these "poems" and rhetoric appears nakedly beneath it.

It should surprise no one that poems which are so rhetorical in purpose and address as those we have been discussing should also be rhetorical in method, but distinction in method between rhetorical and poetic discourse is much less clear-cut than distinction of purpose and address. To become aware of the rhetorical it will help to recall several truisms about rhetoric: (1) that in deliberative or forensic speeches, where persuasion is the chief end, an underlying logical structure can often be seen in a chain of enthymemes, as well as in a relatively formal division into exordium, narration, proposition, proof, disproof, and peroration; (2) that in epideictic speeches, whose chief purpose is praise or blame, it is unusual to

---

only poems having a definite nationalistic bias. There were many partisan and epideictic pieces on other themes, though those showing nationalistic feeling were undoubtedly the most numerous.

53

find either the enthymeme chain or so elaborate an observance of formal divisions. These same principles apply to the verse of the early national period—the stronger the purpose of persuasion the more one is likely to find the pattern of enthymemes and the use of formalistic divisions.

The fact may be illustrated in a persuasive poem subjected to fairly detailed rhetorical analysis. Freneau's "To the Americans" (1775)[7] provides a good subject (see opposite page).

It can be seen first of all that the poem contains five of the six major divisions of a deliberative oration—narration, proposition, proof, disproof, and peroration—lacking only a formal exordium, an omission permissible to a persuasive speech which has to do with war and the future.

Freneau employs here all three chief means of persuasion—*ethos,* emotional appeals, and an argument proper. First, by assuming the character of a good man, a man his audience can trust and believe, he makes use from the very beginning of *ethos,* which Aristotle calls the most powerful means of persuasion. He espouses the cause of Freedom, Truth, and Justice against the cause of Tyranny, Falsehood, and Injustice. He represents himself as angered by the wanton outrages of Gage and the British king, and he takes care to show that his cause is the same as that of the audience—that he is one of them: "If Britain conquers—*we* exist no more." "Such are the devils that swell *our* souls with rage." His name-calling against the British is justifiable since it is the result of the indignation and righteous anger which any good man (in this case, any American) would feel. His good moral character is further established by his use of statements which resemble maxims or declaration of moral truth:

> No toils should daunt the nervous and the bold,
> They scorn all heat or wave-congealing cold.

Second, he attempts to create the desired emotional responses in his audience by outlining the enormity of their enemy's offenses and by giving an example of British atrocity. In some instances he allays their dread of the foe by calling Gage a "mock-imperial lord," the king a "mere imposter," and the Hessians "slaves that serve a tyrant." In other instances he arouses their fear by reminding them of the terrible consequences of failure. He seeks to render his

7. *Poems,* I, 185-187.

TO THE AMERICANS

ON THE RUMORED APPROACH OF THE HESSIAN FORCES, WALDECKERS, ETC. . . .
OCCASIONED BY GENERAL GAGE'S PROCLAMATION THAT THE PROVINCES WERE
IN A STATE OF REBELLION AND OUT OF THE KING'S PROTECTION. (1775)

Rebels you are—the British champion cries—
Truth, stand thou forth!—and tell the wretch, He lies:—
Rebels!—and see this mock imperial lord
Already threats these rebels with the cord.

*Ethical Appeal Combined
with Calumny and
Prophecy*

The hour draws night, the glass is almost run,
When truth will shine, and ruffiians be undone;
When this base miscreant will forbear to sneer,
And curse his taunts and bitter insults here.

If to controul the cunning of a knave,
Freedom respect, and scorn the name of slave;
If to protect against a tyrant's laws,
And arm for vengeance in a righteous cause,
Be deemed Rebellion—'tis a harmless thing:
This bug-bear name, like death, has lost its sting.

Enthymeme "Definition"

    Americans! at freedom's fane adore!
But trust to Britain, and her flag, no more;
The generous genius of their isle has fled,
And left a mere imposter in his stead.

*Enthymeme "Altered
Choices"*

If conquered, rebels (their Scotch records show),
Receive no mercy from the parent foe;

Enthymeme "Induction"

Nay, even the grave, that friendly haunt of peace,
(Where Nature gives the woes of man to cease,)
Vengeance will search—and buried corpses there

*Sham Enthymeme
"Indignation"*

Be raised, to feast the vultures of the air—
Be hanged on gibbets, such a war they wage—
Such are the devils that swell our souls with rage!

If Britain conquers, help us, heaven, to fly:
Lend us your wings, ye ravens of the sky;—

*Enthymeme "Conse-
quences"*

If Britain conquers—we exist no more;
These lands will redden with their children's gore,
Who, turned to slaves, their fruitless toils will moan,
Toils in these fields that once they called their own!

*Sham Enthymeme
"Indignation"*

    To arms! to arms! and let the murdering sword
Decide who best deserves the hangman's cord:
Nor think the hills of Canada too bleak
When desperate Freedom is the prize you seek;
For that, the call of honour bids you go
O'er frozen lakes and mountains wrapt in snow;
No toils should daunt the nervous and the bold,
They scorn all heat or wave-congealing cold.

Maxim

    Haste!—to your tents in iron fetters bring
These slaves, that serve a tyrant and a king;
So just, so virtuous is your cause, I say,
Hell must prevail if Britain gains the day.

Enthymeme "Opposites"

audience bolder and more courageous by appealing to their sense of honor and by exhorting them to "scorn all heat and wave-congealing cold," holding before them at the same time the dangers they will face if they quit themselves like men.

Third, while establishing himself in their favor, and producing the desired attitude in his audience, he presents his main argument in the form of an enthymematic chain. It is this aspect of the poem which lies closest to rhetorical method. He deals at once with his opponent's argument that Americans are rebels by employing an enthymeme of the refutative type drawn from the *topos* "definition":

> If to controul the cunning of a knave,
> Freedom respect, and scorn the name of slave;
> If to protect against a tyrant's laws,
> And arm for vengeance in a righteous cause,
> Be deemed Rebellion—'tis a harmless thing:
> This bug-bear name, like death has lost its sting.

This argument successfully performs a number of functions: first, it places discredit on the enemy, by minimizing their accusations and by implying once more that they are base and tyrannous; secondly, it encourages the audience by magnifying its cause and justifying its actions; and finally, by its paraphrase of scripture: "This bug-bear name, like death, has lost its sting," it serves to raise the *ethos* of the speaker and the cause he pleads.

Freneau next addresses Americans by apostrophe, employing at the same time another enthymeme drawn from the *topos* "altered choices." He argues that because Britain's former freedom has fled and she has become tyrannous, Americans (who love freedom) no longer owe allegiance to the British crown and are now free to transfer their allegiance to the independent state of their own making.

> Americans! at freedom's fane adore!
> But trust to Britain, and her flag, no more;
> The generous genius of their isle has fled,
> And left a mere imposter in his stead.

The next element in the argument is a combined example, enthymeme, and sham enthymeme,[8] though its function as an example

---

8. A sham enthymeme Aristotle defines as one that looks genuine but is in reality spurious. He lists nine common varieties, the first and perhaps the most common type arising from the structure of the diction in a compact and

is, perhaps, of greatest importance. He warns Americans that they can expect no mercy from their British conquerers, and cites the British treatment of the Scotch rebels who, like the Americans, were closely related to the British. The first part of this argument from example is in the form of an enthymeme drawn from the *topos* "induction."

> If conquered, rebels (their Scotch records show),
> Receive no mercy from the parent foe.

What follows resembles a sham enthymeme of the type called by Aristotle "indignation." "Such means," he says, "are used when the speaker, without having proved his case, elaborates on the nature of the deed." Freneau has stated that the British are cruel to conquered rebels and has supported his statement by reference to their behavior towards the Scotch. He then elaborates, employing more "indignation" and imagination than facts:

> Nay, even the grave, that friendly haunt of peace,
> (Where Nature gives the woes of man to cease,)
> Vengeance will search—and buried corpses there
> Be raised, to feast the vultures of the air—
> Be hanged on gibbets, such a war they wage—
> Such are the devils that swell our souls with rage!

The next enthymeme, "If Britain conquers—we exist no more," is drawn from the *topos* "consequences," and enlarges upon an already established idea, the ferocity of the British as conquerors. And following this, Freneau uses another sham enthymeme of the same sort he has already used, by elaborating upon the consequences of an event which has not yet occurred:

> These lands will redden with their children's gore,
> Who, turned to slaves, their fruitless toils will moan,
> Toils in these fields that once they called their own.

Appropriately, he has reserved his strongest appeal for action

---

antithetical statement. Such sham enthymemes appear especially when a speaker summarizes the results of his previous arguments, the juxtaposition of several conclusions appearing to prove something about another conclusion. Aristotle cites an example of this from Isocrates' *Evagoras:* "Some he saved"; "others he avenged"; "he liberated Greece." Each of these points has been proved from something else; when they are brought together, they seem to establish a novel conclusion. *Rhetoric,* 1401a.

until the issues have been painted in the bold colors of his own choosing. For now he appeals to his audience by direct apostrophe, as if the time for speaking were past and the time for drastic action had come. He draws his appeal from the *topos* "turning one's opponent's own words against him":

> To arms! to arms! and let the murdering sword
> Decide who best deserves the hangman's cord.

His exhortation continues, after an appeal to honor, with a strong imperative:

> Haste!—to your tents in iron fetters bring
> These slaves, that serve a tyrant and a king.

The last two lines in the poem are an enthymeme from the *topos* "opposites" employing both antithesis and hyperbole for the final emotional appeal:

> So just, so virtuous is your cause, I say,
> Hell must prevail if Britain gains the day.

In this persuasive poem Freneau has consistently followed the method of deliberative rhetoric—whether consciously, as if with rhetorical text open in one hand, or unconsciously, drawing upon intuitive resources or previous academic training, it is hard to say in the absence of external evidence. In any case, the poem illustrates the principle that in most of the partisan and epideictic poetry of the period there is a visible use of rhetorical method in proportion to the amount of persuasion.

Even the epideictic verse sometimes shows an attachment to its own rhetorical prescriptions of form. In classical rhetoric epideictic speeches, because they had no developed argument, dropped away the divisions of proposition, proof, or disproof, and were commonly divided into exordium, an extended narration which comprised the main body of the speech, and a peroration, with some varieties of epideictic having their own conventional divisions. Encomium of person, for example, had exordium, peroration, and six named subdivisions of narration.[9] Apparently the poets of the early national period were acquainted with these conventions, for occasion-

9. For a thorough, scholarly treatment of this mode of discourse see Theodore C. Burgess, *Epideictic Literature, University of Chicago Studies in Classical Philology*, III (1902).

ally some elegiac poem like Robert Treat Paine's "A Monody to the Memory of W. H. Brown" will show many of these parts (Paine's shows six).[10] But encomia of this kind are rare among the other epideictic poems which are more likely to resemble Francis Scott Key's "The Star Spangled Banner" (1814), a poem mainly epideictic but having a minor deliberative element. Such pieces are usually organized according to some loose sequence of narrative or description with here and there a hortatory enthymeme, but they seldom have any carefully articulated skeleton of argument. This is not to say that such poems are not rhetorical, for most of them are highly rhetorical in other ways than method.

Posterity has unknowingly separated the epideictic and partisan poems from the other poetry of this period. Verse which those poets took most seriously (the part we have just been describing) posterity has rejected—the poems which helped to win the Revolution have not been able to win the hearts of succeeding generations. Almost the only poems much honored today either by the critics or by the anthologists are those which were considered by their makers as "minor" verse, those which carry little overt doctrine, serve no utilitarian purpose, and are freest from attachment to particular audience and occasion. Barlow's "Hasty Pudding," Trumbull's "Progress of Dulness," and Freneau's nature lyrics are among such poems. Without knowing either these poets or their work, Goethe accurately pronounced their fate in the last of his conversations with Eckermann: "If a poet would work politically, he must give himself up to a party; and as soon as he does that, he is lost as a poet."

10. *Works*, pp. 118-121. A poem which shows Paine following with even greater fidelity the classical prescriptions for encomium of a person is his "Monody on the Death of Lieutenant General Sir John Moore." *Works*, pp. 229-236. See also "An Elegy on a Patriot" from Book XII of the *Anarchiad* for a mock elegy containing a number of the classical prescriptions for encomium.

6. POETRY BY
FORMULA: STYLE

In one of the early chapters of *The Last of the Mohicans* Hawkeye makes this pledge to help Cora and Alice Munro escape from hostile Indians: "These Mohicans and I will do what man's thoughts can invent, to keep such flowers, which, though so sweet, were never made for the wilderness, from harm, and that without hope of any other recompense but such as God always gives to upright dealings." Hearing such pompous language from a supposedly unlettered scout, modern readers can hardly suppress a smile. We associate such language with the posturing and extravagance of the old melodramas, or with charlatanry, as in the movie scene where W. C. Fields as patent-medicine salesman at the tail gate of his wagon bamboozles the yokels with fancy talk. But if such talk strikes us as openly false, we have no reason to believe that it troubled Cooper's readers in any such way, or even that Hawthorne's readers as late as 1860 found the same formality of style in *The Marble Faun* unduly stiff or artificial. The truth is that Americans of the early nineteenth century were conditioned to an extravagance of style both in prose and poetry which modern taste condemns as outrageously "rhetorical." We have come now to the point where we must face the term "rhetorical," not in the meanings which refer to persuasive purpose or restricted audience or occasion, but in the common pejorative meaning which refers to artificially heightened style, a meaning to which the early national poetry seems particularly vulnerable.

We begin with "the rules," which laid an unusually heavy hand upon American poetic practice. Long after the spirit of Augustan orthodoxy had been diluted or eclipsed in England by other criteria of literary excellence, it still dominated critical thinking in America. As late as 1807 *The Monthly Anthology and Boston Review* could claim that, "The rules of verse were formed out of the experience of poets, and are necessary to the composition of poetry. It is not to render service to genius to disengage it from subjection to method. . . . Poems will please only in proportion as these rules are observed."[1] Poets and critics alike (there was little distinction

1. III, 121.

between the two) accepted all the common assumptions of neo-classic criticism: the *ut pictura poesis* of Horace, the insistence upon "pure" diction and "smooth" numbers, the belief that all the best themes as well as the choicest figures and other ornaments had already been used by the great poets of the past and that the contemporary poet could do little more than reshuffle these known elements into new and pleasing combinations. As the English Augustans had turned to Rome and to France for models of classic excellence, the American poets tourned to Pope. "Since the days of Pope," said one critic in 1805, "this species of excellence [smoothness of numbers] has become almost mechanical. The artisan of verses has only to resort to his work, in which . . . may be found every musical and every graceful phrase, which our language affords, and the manufacture of harmonious lines becomes the easiest thing in the world."[2] Those two phrases, "the artisan of verses," and "the manufacture of harmonious lines," express completely the dominant spirit of this poetry.

Both critics and poets were preoccupied with the externals of poetry—with versification, diction, figures, technique in general—the aspects of poetry upon which rules were most binding. Like the Augustans, they looked upon these as "ornaments," as the "enamel," "painting," or "colors" which a poet could apply, as it were, from the outside, which could be manipulated or revised according to rules which had no reference to the inner intent of a particular poem. So strong was this preoccupation with method and reason that some voices were raised in protest: "The times of inspiration are departed; and nature, the only muse of the poet, is unfeelingly forgotten. We have substituted rhetoric in her room and degenerated to a race of manufacturers."[3]

If such mechanical tendencies can be traced to Augustan practice or precept, there was little in Blair and the other Scots of the later eighteenth century—as Americans read them—which would discourage their growth. The tenacity of older neoclassicism is clearly seen in Blair's *Lectures*, where a number of the basic principles of classicism were preserved fairly intact, even though they were bedfellows of new and revolutionary ideas.[4] As a member of the Scot-

2. *Monthly Anthology*, II (1805), 380.
3. *Ibid.*, p. 530.
4. Cf. Walter J. Bate, *From Classic to Romantic* (Cambridge, Mass., 1946), p. 113.

tish "Common-Sense School," Blair received a marked influence from the Shaftesburyan conceptions of the innate moral sense, the interest in associational psychology, and the strong empirical sense which are among the characteristics of this group. In his *Lectures on Rhetoric and Belles-Lettres* his emphasis is on taste, on the sublime and sublimity in writing, and on style. These aspects of his book display tendencies toward relativism in taste, toward subjectivity and an emphasis on the particular which are quite to be expected from a member of the Common-Sense School. But these tendencies are not pure. The older neoclassic predilection for rules survives in the midst of them, the same arbitrariness, the same uniformitarian assumption that a norm is possible and desirable through the exercise of reason. Blair's rules may have been different from those of Boileau and Pope, somewhat diluted by new-fangled ideas, but it is clear that he felt it proper and even necessary to formulate rules. The codification that was so characteristic of neoclassicism Blair applied, like Kames before him and Alison after him, to taste and the sublime as well as to the other areas of poetic theory which had conventionally been "methodized"; and thus he widened, rather than narrowed, for his followers the varieties and aspects of poetry which could be produced by formula. Although Kames and Blair set up their rules less on the authority of ancient practice and precept than on an analysis of the taste of the generality of mankind, this made their rules no less arbitrary and rationalistic. Kames said that his intention was to show how "the fine arts, like morals, become a rational science," how "criticism could be rational."[5] This approach Blair followed closely, and there are many signs that the subjectivity, the relativity of taste, and the Shaftesburyan "enthusiasm" in the Scottish rhetorics received far less attention from Americans than the prescriptive portions of these works. Kames and Blair ordinarily stood for "the rules" to Americans, and Blair especially after 1785 was deferred to as an authority in literary matters.[6]

We have seen that verse was the chief distinction which this generation allowed between rhetoric and poetic, and no one could deny that the style of their poems is uncompromisingly poetic in its fondness for the neoclassic couplet. Their pieces look and sound

5. *Elements of Criticism*, Chapter 1.
6. See a review of Blair's *Lectures* in the *New Haven Gazette and Connecticut Magazine*, I (1786), 107.

like poems. But even in cherishing such external marks of poetic style, the poets only succeeded in casting sheep's clothing over the rhetorical wolf which crept into the poetic fold anyway, not only through the doors of purpose and address but also through style itself, for many of the rules which they followed with such slavish confidence derived ultimately from Roman rhetoric and always retained the spirit of their origin.

One of the most pervasive influences came from the ancient rhetorical concept of three styles. Cicero had assigned to oratory the threefold function of *docere, conciliare,* and *movere* ("to teach," "to please," and "to move"), and to each of these functions he had assigned one of the three styles, *tenue, medium,* and *grande.*[7] Throughout the Middle Ages and the Renaissance and on into the neoclassic age this threefold division continued to be observed. In the eighteenth century Cicero's *tenue* was usually translated as the "low" or "simple" style; *medium* became the "middle" or "mixed" or "florid" style; and *grande* became the "high," the "grand," or the "sublime" style. The Scottish rhetoricians extended this division far beyond style until it constituted a virtual threefold division of all discourse. An American disciple of the Scottish school (John Witherspoon) allowed to the grand style epic poetry, tragedy, and orations on grand subjects; to the "simple" style he allowed scientific writing, epistolary writing, essay, dialogue, and epitaph; to the mixed or middle style, he allowed "history, system, and controversy." He also made a distinction between "sentiment" and "language," giving a classic example of what T. S. Eliot meant by the "dissociation of sensibility." Witherspoon claimed that pieces intended for the high style should be sublime in both sentiment and language, that pieces in the simple style might often be sublime in sentiment but rarely in language, and that in the mixed-style pieces might be either simple or sublime both in sentiment and in language.[8]

But more often than not, when an American poet composed a poem, the decision about which style he would use had already been made for him by some such precept. The simple style, which avoided figures, used the shortest, plainest words, and attempted

7. *Orator,* trans. H. M. Hubbell (Cambridge, 1931), XXI, 69-71. Cf. C. S. Baldwin, *Ancient Rhetoric and Poetic,* pp. 250-251.

8. *Lectures on Moral Philosophy and Eloquence* (Woodward's 3rd ed., Philadelphia, 1810), p. 195.

an easy direct manner. This style can be seen in some of Freneau's best lyrics, such as "The Wild Honeysuckle," or in his fine elegy "On the Death of Franklin" which has the compactness and restraint of classical epigram. Dwight's *Greenfield Hill* provides a good example of a poem in the middle style, which avoided "low" words and made much use of *periphrasis*, poetic diction, and *hypotyposis* or vivid description. It is not the poems in these styles, however, which strike us as "rhetorical," as much as it is the many poems which attempt the high or sublime style. Eighteenth-century poets generally regarded sublimity as the highest pinnacle on the Parnassian mount, a height which only the loftiest genius could attain, though the theorists considered that they had at least charted a path thither by their canons of rules governing the sublime. The American poets, even without the strong pinions of genius, often attempted to soar to the sublime heights by an observance of these rules, and while their determination was admirable, and while there was much noisy and gaudy flapping of wings, they never flew very high.

There are good reasons why the cult of the sublime, which was one of the chief esthetic movements in the eighteenth century set against the domination of reason, should be one more force to turn American poetic expression in a rhetorical direction. For one thing, as Samuel H. Monk has shown in his authoritative study, eighteenth-century theories of the sublime were deeply rooted in classical rhetoric and they never entirely lost a coloring from this rhetorical source.[9] The *Peri Hupsous,* the source of most of these theories, is primarily a rhetorical treatise, based on the division of expression into three styles. Longinus was chiefly concerned with the grand style, to which the ancients had assigned the purpose of arousing emotion in an audience, and which they had usually reserved for the peroration or for the parts of a speech intended to be especially forceful. This was the style which eighteenth-century theorists, following Longinus, felt to be appropriate to the sublime.

Eighteenth-century discussions recognized two chief variations of the sublime: (1) the rhetorical sublime, which was characterized by the assumption that the emotions have a practical value in

9. *The Sublime, A Study of Critical Theories in Eighteenth Century England* (New York, 1935). The extensive debt to Monk of the subsequent discussion of the sublime will be plain to all who are familiar with his excellent study.

persuading an audience against the reason and will, (2) the pathetic or esthetic sublime, in which the emotions as a source of esthetic pleasure were the center of attention. The first type remained closely associated with rhetoric, its chief sign being the grand style described by Longinus. The second type became during the eighteenth century a generalized concept applying to all the arts, and led to the formulation of the conditions and even the classes of objects which could produce the particular emotional effects thought to be the basis of both types of the sublime. S. H. Monk's chief interest is in the esthetic sublime, especially as it led into romanticism, but he freely admits the importance of rhetoric even to this branch of theory.[10]

Although Longinus and Edmund Burke were studied in the colleges, Americans derived their ideas of the sublime chiefly through Kames and Blair. Both of these men gave extensive catalogs of the elements of the sublime; Blair's listing will be quoted here because it is somewhat fuller and more compact than Kames', though it differs in no other important respect.

Blair spoke of the impression of the sublime on the mind as being "wonder and astonishments . . . a degree of awfulness and solemnity, even approaching to severity," and of the things which produce it as being chiefly "the vast and boundless prospects of nature, extended plains, the expanse of the ocean, the unlimited heavens, high mountains to which we look up, or an awful precipice or tower whence we look down. . . . Remove all bounds from any object and you presently render it sublime." Hence infinite space, endless numbers, and eternal duration fill the mind with great ideas. Loudness of sound, too, is capable of producing sublimity. "The burst of thunder or of cannons, the roaring of winds, the shouting of multitudes, the sound of vast cataracts of water, are all incontestibly grand objects." Power and force are capable of raising sublime ideas; such things as earthquakes, volcanoes, great fires, stormy seas, hurricanes, thunder and lightning, roaring floods, show that "nothing is more sublime than mighty power and strength."[11]

American poets ordinarily sought to achieve the sublime in their poetry by inserting with studied frequency these recognizable elements. Note how many are used by Freneau in this passage from "The House of Night" (1779):

10. Monk, p. 235.
11. *Lectures,* III.

65

Dark was the sky and not one friendly star
Shone from the zenith, or horizon, clear,
Mist sate upon the woods, and *darkness rode
In her black chariot, with a wild career.*

And from the woods the late resounding note
Issued of the loquacious Whip-poor-will,
*Hoarse, howling dogs, and nightly-roving wolves
Clamour'd from far off cliffs invisible.*

Rude, from the *wide-extended Chesapeake*
I heard *the winds the dashing waves assail,*
And saw *from far,* by picturing fancy form's
The *black ship* travelling through *the noisy gale.*[12]

Or note the following passage, selected virtually at random from Dwight's *Conquest of Canaan:*

Far distant, Zimri, *like a sweeping storm,*
Grim in the chariot rais'd *his gloomy form;*
Earth shook, air trembled, heaven with thunder roar'd:
Oft, from the car descending to the plain,
He steamed, like lightning, (o'er the *ghastly* slain),
Then *swiftly rose,* and on the heathens *sped,*
His wheels *dark-rolling o'er th' unnumber'd dead.*[13]

The theories of associational psychology which lay behind the esthetics of the Scottish rhetoricians assumed that most men would have essentially the same responses to natural phenomena: for example, the primary sensation in all men at the sight of a vast, craggy mountain would be wonder or awe and a feeling of elevation. From this it was easy to infer that in order to achieve sublime effects a poet had only to bring before the reader objects or phenomena which were known to evoke awe and elevation. The means to do this was the grand or sublime style, and the rules governing this style were many and definite.

While Kames and Blair were substantially in agreement as to the elements of the sublime, there was some difference of emphasis in their recommendations for achieving it. As the later of the two men, Blair, when he wrote his *Lectures,* was drawing away from the concept of sublimity as residing principally in the grand style and was inclining toward the wider concept of the esthetic sub-

12. *Poems,* I, 214-215. Italics added.   13. Book VIII. Italics added.

lime in which attention was centered on the emotions themselves. Possibly under the influence of Ossian, Blair was quite outspoken in his condemnation of the "sublime style"—the "magnificent words, accumulated epithets, and a certain swelling kind of expression." For Blair sublimity resided in the thought, not in the words, "and when the thought is truly noble, it will for the most part clothe itself in a native dignity of language. . . ." The main secret of being sublime is to say things in few and plain words. The true sublime comes not "by hunting after tropes and figures and rhetorical assistance. . . . It stands clear, for the most part, of these laboured refinements of art. It must come unsought if it comes at all; and be the natural offspring of a strong imagination." He quoted, after Longinus, these lines from Genesis as a good example of sublimity residing in simple words: "God said, let there be light; and there was light." Then he added, "This is striking and sublime. But put it into what is commonly called the sublime styles: 'The sovereign arbiter of nature, by the potent energy of a single word, commanded the light to exist'; and . . . the style is indeed raised, but the thought is fallen."[14]

Kames retained much more of Longinus' idea that sublimity resides in elevated style. His capital rule for reaching the sublime was that the poet should strive for "grandeur of manner" by presenting "those parts or circumstances only which make the greatest figure, keeping out of view everything low or trivial." He said also that "a man, when elevated or animated by passion, is disposed to elevate or animate all his objects: he avoids familiar names, exalts objects by circumlocution and metaphor. . . . In this heat of mind the highest poetical flights are indulged. . . . An elevated subject requires an elevated style. . . . Nothing contributes more than inversion to the force and elevation of language."[15] The sublime style according to Kames made much use of all the heightening devices: circumlocution, inversion, epithet, poetic diction, figures— especially the strong figures of hyperbole, personification, apostrophe, and interrogation. Even Blair, though he warned against the overuse of such devices, enumerated and discussed them all.

Most of these means of obtaining sublime style were included in "amplification," a quality plainly visible in this poetical paraphrase of Genesis by Timothy Dwight:

14. *Lectures*, IV.   15. *Elements of Criticism*, Chapter 4.

[And the earth was without form and void; and darkness was upon the face of the deep. Genesis 1:2.]

> From realms divine, high raised beyond all height,
> Th' Almighty Parent cast his piercing sight,
> With boundless view, he saw the etherial vast
> A clouded gloom, an undelightsome waste:
> Around the extended wild, no sun's broad ray
> Mark'd the clear splendor of immortal day;
> No varying moon, ordain'd at eve to rise,
> Led the full pomp of the constelleate skies;
> No day in circling beauty learn'd to roll;
> Substantial darkness space unmeasur'd fill'd,
> And nature's realm lay desolate and wild.[16]

Dwight was writing, as Leon Howard has shown, directly under the influence of Kames, and following with great fidelity his precepts for achieving the sublime.[17] But for a reader to have anything like a true idea of such "sublime" verse, the copiousness within this passage must be seen as multiplied over and over again. The American poets followed with fatal fidelity Kames' rule that "grandeur, being an extreme vivid emotion, is not readily produced in perfection but by reiterated impressions. The effect of a single impression can be but momentary. . . . Successive images, making thus deeper and deeper impressions, must elevate more than any single image can do."[18] They were so prodigal with their sublime passages that the reader soon becomes wearied and oppressed by the unrelenting assault on his sensations of passages which break over him, wave after wave, seeming to let up only to gather strength for another assault. This prodigality helps to explain why most events in their poetry, especially in the epics, have the aspect of major cataclysms—they believed that by hitting the reader again and again on the same nerve they would increase the degree of sublimity in the poem.

The more one reads this verse, the more he is led to the conclusion that it was not the theories themselves—even though they had origins in rhetoric—which chiefly gave such verse its "rhetorical" cast. If the handbooks methodized sublime objects and emotions, thus making them available to any poetaster, they also gave

16. *Columbian Muse,* pp. 196-198.
17. Howard, *The Connecticut Wits,* Chapters 3 and 4.
18. *Elements of Criticism,* Chapter 4.

ample warning against the pitfalls of the false sublime. What chiefly was at fault was that American poets, ignoring the warnings and finding justification in the assumptions of a mechanistic psychology, went on to write in the sublime style anyway. If the sublime could not be made to grow naturally out of their verse, they would freight it in from the outside. The rhetoricians called for heightened passion to lend elevation to poetry, but of course they meant that the poet's own passions must be aroused. All too often the passion in these poems is purely external, not necessarily experienced by the poet at all, the assumption being that simply by depicting strong emotion the poet would lend the desired elevation to the poem.

An article published in the *Boston Magazine* for 1784 gives a clear picture of the attitude which lay behind much of the sublime poetry of this period. The author proposes an ode on Niagara Falls—a subject particularly suited to sublime effects:

The poem might open with a general description of the country, and sure no country allows fuller scope to the descriptive powers —here everything is majestic and truly natural; then might follow a particular account of the stupendous cataract. . . . The contemplation of this immense spectacle, considered with these attendant circumstances, cannot fail of raising lofty and sublime ideas in any one possessed of poetic fire and fancy. Some beautiful and affecting tale might also be built upon that well-known truth, that the Indians in attempting to cross the flood above the cataract, are often hurried into eternity by the impetuous current. We may suppose the sufferer to have been a favorite chief or bosom friend, and may easily conceive what would be the expressions of grief among a people whose passions civilization had not yet put under any restraint, but who are guided solely by the impulse of nature and instinct—I know not but their attachment to a leader and companion might induce many to plunge into the roaring flood, to accompany him in his solitary journey to the land of spirits, *at least this is a circumstance of which the poet might allowedly avail himself to heighten the scene.*[19]

This writer reflects the urgent feeling so common at the time that America ought to be producing poetry in the grand manner. Clearly he assumes that the vast spectacle of Niagara Falls, or violent death from being swept over the falls, or the extreme grief

19. *Boston Magazine*, I (1784), 196.

which might drive a man to suicide are circumstances "of which the poet might allowedly avail himself to heighten the scene." Sublimity apparently could be brought coolly into the poem from the outside.

The other common means of injecting the sufficient degree of passion to produce the sublime in a poem was to resort to the strong figures—personification, apostrophe, hyperbole, exclamation, interrogation, and the numerous variations of these figures. Especially overworked was a type of personification which Blair called the strongest of all figures of speech, that "in which inanimate objects are introduced not only as feeling and acting, but also as speaking to us, or hearing and listening when we address ourselves to them."[20] This figure and the one closely related to it, apostrophe, were used in such excess that they might be regarded as hallmarks of American poetry during this period. Humphreys, in his "Poem on the Industry of the United States" (1794), apostrophizes or personifies in twenty pages of verse forty-two separate persons, places, or things, ranging from "Genius of Culture!" to "Lusitania, queen of diamond mines!" And this does not include the many instances of *exclamatio* like "Heavens!" "Ho!" "Ah!" and the like.[21]

If these figures were used often in didactic and epic verse which aspired to the sublime, they were used even more in the epideictic verse where there were special sanctions for extravagant utterance. The ancient rhetoricians had plainly said that "the function of panegyric is to amplify and embellish its themes."[22] Besides this, the ode throughout the neoclassic period, particularly the pseudo-pindaric of Cowley, had been allowed excesses of expression which were given to no other type of poetry. Blair spoke of "that enthusiasm which is understood to be a characteristic of lyric poetry." He said that "a professed ode, even of the moral kind, but more especially if its attempts the sublime, is expected to be enlivened and animated in an unusual degree."[23] He conceived of the ode as retaining many qualities of primitive bardic poetry, which he

20. *Lectures,* XVI.
21. See Parrington, *The Connecticut Wits,* pp. 385-405.
22. Quintilian, *Institutio Oratoria,* III, vii, 6.
23. *Lectures,* XXXIX. For a detailed study of the ode in English literature during the neoclassic period see George N. Shuster, *The English Ode from Milton to Keats,* in *Columbia University Studies in English and Comparative Literature,* No. 150 (New York, 1940).

described as being virtually indistinguishable from oratory. Primitive poetry was full of "wild and disordered strains," because in the earliest time "history, eloquence, and poetry were all the same."[24]

American poets took all the liberties allowed by the theorists. They packed their odes with apostrophes and personifications; they used every trick for attaining a high style, and these poems show even more than the attempts at epic the worst effects of having been composed by a perfunctory observance of formulae.[25] All too often their earnestness led them to use the strong figures without regard to whether they belonged in a particular context. William Livingston in his poem called "Philosophic Solitude" begs the muses to guide him to quiet sequestered scenes, but having arrived at those scenes, he shatters the quiet by hailing them in stentorian tones:

> Me to sequestered scenes, ye muses, guide,
> Where nature wantons in her virgin pride. . . .
> Welcome, ye shades! all hail, ye vernal blooms!
> Ye bow'ry thickets, and prophetic glooms!
> Ye forests, Hail! ye solitary woods!
> Love-whispering groves, and silver-streaming floods!
> Ye birds, and all ye sylvan beauties hail!
> Oh how I long with you to spend my days,
> I invoke the muse and try the rural lays![26]

Several influences outside the literary tradition itself encouraged the excesses of emotion and the perfunctory observance of formulae so evident in the poetry. Of these the mechanical drilling in elocution must have been one. It is hard to believe that poetry so full of the histrionic tags "Lo, here!" "Lo, there!" "Methinks I see . . . methinks I hear!" "But, ah!"—and so thoroughly larded with the exclamatory figures—is not under strong influence from elocution. Too many of the poems seem to have been written to give a declaimer the greatest possible chance to exercise his talents in the

24. *Lectures*, VI, XXXVIII.
25. For examples look almost at random in Robert Treat Paine's *Works*.
26. *Columbian Muse*, p. 17. For a spirited objection by Freneau to such excesses see *Poems*, III, 235-237. See also *ibid.*, p. 38; and an article in *Massachusetts Magazine*, VIII (1796), 477, in which one critic lists as "Directions for Composing an Elegy" all the most common clichés and abuses. Other complaints about the excesses of epideictic poetry are to be found in *The New Haven Gazette and Connecticut Magazine*, I (1786), 145-147; *Monthly Magazine and American Review*, II (1800), 309; *Port Folio*, II (1802), 195; *Monthly Anthology and Boston Review*, II (1805), 305; VIII (1810), 257-258.

extravagant gesture and the posturing of this kind of speaking. There is one other respect in which the elocution manuals might have exerted influence on the poetry. The descriptions of passion in the poetry closely resemble those in Burgh and the other elocution manuals. Note how Dwight's description of fear in one of his epic villains compares with Burgh's description of fear in the introductory chapter to his *Art of Speaking:*

> In dread amaze astonish'd Samlah stood;
> From his pale face retired the freezing blood;
> His wild eye star'd; all bristling rose his hair;
> Quick from his quivering hand the useless spear
> Dropp'd; his teeth rattled, and the falling reins
> At random trembled on the coursers' manes;
> Behind he gaz'd and found no path to fly;
> For aid he panted, but no aid was nigh.[27]

Fear, violent and sudden, opens very wide the eyes and mouth; shortens the nose; draws down the eyebrows; gives the countenance an air of wildness; covers it with deadly paleness. . . . The body seems shrinking from the danger and putting itself in a posture for flight. The heart beats violently; the breath is fetched quick and short; the whole body is thrown in a general tremor. The voice is weak and trembling.[28]

It would be absurd to claim that Dwight learned these characteristics of the passion of fear solely from Burgh, though the similarity in such a wide coverage of detail is striking. It seems reasonable that a book like Burgh's, the subject of intensive study in the schools, should exert some influence over the literary habits of the students, especially when it is recalled that most of the recitation of poems and speeches was by rote, the student memorizing the appropriate gestures and signs of emotion along with the words of the poem or speech. Thus Burgh and the other manuals of elocution furnished another store of ready-made materials which could be put to use by the aspiring poet. It did not matter if these materials were familiar to the point of triteness; mechanical methods

27. *The Conquest of Canaan,* Book VIII.
28. Burgh, p. 21. The art of gesture in elocution had itself become so refined that whole treatises were devoted to it. See, for example, Gilbert Austin, *Chironomia* (London, 1806), in which separate chapters were devoted to positions of the feet and legs, positions and movements of the arms, hands, head, eyes, shoulders, and other chapters to the stroke and time of gestures, the preparation and transition of gesture, and the like.

72

in poetry were not unusual in America at this time and originality was not the poetic virtue most sought after.

The widespread training in elocution was not the only external influence which encouraged extravagance in the poetry. This was an age when bombast was characteristic of many forms of prose writing, especially of the prose orations. Excesses in the poetry are more understandable when it is remembered that audiences habitually listened to speeches as unbelievably bombastic as the following "Oration on the History, Culture and Qualities of the Potatoe," which was delivered at the public commencement exercises of the University of Pennsylvania in 1790:

Farmers of Pennsylvania, cultivate the potatoe! Citizens of Philadelphia, eat, oh! eat, plentifully and constantly of the potatoe! Let them be the constant food of your children, instead of bread, in the intervals of their meals. Legislators of Pennsylvania encourage by suitable bounties, the increase and exportation of the potatoe. Let this precious root be blended hereafter with the wheat-sheaf, in the arms of our State. [Here Mr. Bache took a potatoe from his pocket and held it in his hand.] Hail highly favored vegetable! parent of health, strength, courage, and beauty of the human species! nay more, parent of the human species themselves! may we always honour thee! and may we always eat thee, as we should do! with meat or without it, with butter-milk or without it; in soup, in puddings, in pies, in bread, in biscuit, in sage, in salad, or in coffee!—Still may we prefer thee to all other vegetables! Sweet root! kind root! I take thee to my bosom; go people our western country, [Here the potatoe was gently thrown on the stage, and viewed affectionately in pronouncing the remaining part of the oration.] go teach the nations of the earth to be temperate and healthy, go civilize the world.[29]

There is no indication that the audience even smiled at this performance, nor any reason why they should have, when this student orator was only riding the well-grooved track of received taste in speaking.

Nor was extravagance of style confined to speechmaking. Dr. Joseph Brown Ladd in 1786 found in America "a general depravation of style . . . in which sound has been substituted for sense, and tinsel for ornament. . . . In their attempt to achieve the sublime they have only combined the florid and bombastic manner.

29. *Universal Asylum and Columbian Magazine*, V (1790), 234.

This we would choose to call the frothy manner."[30] Other critics made similar comments about the prose style: "There is a bombast which characterizes and disgraces most of the ephemeral productions of our infant republic."[31] "The orators of the day have too often substituted the vagaries of imagination for the deduction of reason, unnatural conceits for appropriate embellishments, and the rant of enthusiasm for salutary exhortation"[32]—a blast not entirely free from the elaborate style it castigates. With so much bombast on all sides in the prose, it is easy to understand how the poetry could be infected with it.

Now finally to answer the question with which we started—in what ways is the style of this poetry "rhetorical"? It must be said in all fairness that it is rhetorical only in certain special senses. These poets followed the rules slavishly, and much of their verse seems to us highly extravagant in style. Yet there is nothing in the observance of rules of style which by itself will make poetry rhetorical. Grammar, syntax, imagery, diction, figures, rhythm—all the elements of style belong as much to poetry as to rhetoric. They are usually thought of as rhetorical because they have been formulated not by poets but by rhetoricians who have been concerned to codify the "available means of persuasion" so that these means could be taught to students of the art of persuasion. This reflects the rationalistic attitude which prevails in rhetoric, the assumption that the orator must know all the means of persuasion so that he may select and apply the means which are most effective in a given case. Bombast and other stylistic excesses have been considered "rhetorical" because they are characteristic of sophistic rhetoric, the type of rhetoric in which style was of chief importance. Because the rhetoric of style was so long dominant (in England it was

30. "Critical Reflections on Style," *American Museum or Universal Magazine,* I (1787), 532-536, reprinted in *Massachusetts Magazine,* IV (1792), 237-239.   31. *Port Folio,* V (1805), 249.

32. *Ibid.,* p. 221. See for similar remarks *ibid.,* II (1802), 138; new [3rd] series, V (1810), 45-46; VII (1812), 6. "The Echo," by two of the Connecticut Wits, Richard Alsop and Theodore Dwight, published in some twenty numbers of the *American Mercury* (1791-1805), was originally intended to satirize bad taste in contemporary American writing. The earlier numbers, before it turned its attention chiefly to politics, carried out this aim. The usual technique was to reprint some especially bombastic or objectionable passage from a current newspaper and then write a burlesque poem on it. The first "Echo," for example, had good fun burlesquing the grand manner of the false sublime employing all the standard devices of heightened style to describe the burning of a hay barn.

dominant till the middle of the seventeenth century), the word "rhetoric" often has connoted excesses in style, and has carried with it some of the bad ethical reputation of the sophists. It is chiefly in this pejorative sense of the word that the style of American poetry of the early national period is "rhetorical"; it is "mere" rhetoric in the sense that it emphasizes style at the expense of thought and truth. We should add that it is by no means always rhetorical in this sense. Partisan poems like Freneau's "To The Americans," though they may appear exclamatory to modern taste, often employ a blunt and vigorous style quite appropriate to their persuasive purpose, and their style can therefore be seen as rhetorical in the good sense that it constitutes an additional means of persuasion. In the same way the much greater extravagance in the sublime and the epideictic verse can be seen as legitimate—up to a point—since these poets felt they were working within the received conventions of the high style. Modern judgment is particularly harsh on the epideictic verse because the whole mode and the rules which governed it have passed out of ken.

But not even these qualifications will take off the curse. The style of this verse still seems "rhetorical" in the bad sense, and to find an answer to the question of why, we are driven back to the poets themselves and their stance toward the rules. Here we find strong reminders of rhetoric. These poets selected and applied laws of style to achieve desired poetic effects in the same rationalistic way an orator might select particular means of persuasion. Most of the great poets of antiquity, to say nothing of Dante, Spenser, and Milton, observed essentially the same laws of style, but their poetry is not often damned as being "mere" rhetoric. The difference is that American poets of this period wrote by rule only. Their poems were usually artifacts, sometimes constructed with great ingenuity, but more often loosely pasted together from known elements. Only rarely were they, like the poems of Milton, new and original products, created by a refusion of these elements. American poems of this period are often "mere" rhetoric in the sense that they are mere stylistic, lacking the illumination which can come only from a radiant inner core of poetic imagination and emotion.

BIBLIOGRAPHICAL NOTE

The present study ranged perforce through several fields in establishing its conclusions, and made use of so many materials of different kinds that a full listing would run to prohibitive length. The footnotes to the various chapters should give a glimpse of the sources used in the separate sections of the study. In the following bibliographical note my intention is to describe the chief primary sources in American poetry and literary criticism of the early national period, and to present a highly selective list of other books which were of primary importance in completing the study.

The poetry subjected to close scrutiny was chiefly the verse of Freneau in *The Poems of Philip Freneau, Poet of the Revolution*, edited by Fred L. Pattee, Princeton, 1902-1907, 3 vols., this supplemented by *The Last Poems of Philip Freneau*, edited by Lewis Leary, New Brunswick, N. J., 1946; Joel Barlow, *The Vision of Columbus*, Hartford, 1787, *The Hasty Pudding*, New Haven, 1796, *The Columbiad*, Baltimore, 1807; David Humphreys, *Poems by David Humphreys*, Philadelphia, 1789, *The Miscellaneous Works of Colonel David Humphreys*, New York, 1790; Timothy Dwight, *The Conquest of Canaan; a Poem in Eleven Books*, Hartford, 1785, *The Triumph of Infidelity: a Poem*, n.p., 1788, *Greenfield Hill: a Poem in Seven Parts*, New York, 1794; John Trumbull, *The Poetical Works of John Trumbull*, Hartford, 1820, 2 vols.; Francis Hopkinson, *Science: a Poem*, Philadelphia, 1762, *The Battle of the Kegs*, Philadelphia, 1779, *Account of the Grand Federal Procession: an Ode*, Philadelphia, 1788, *Ode From Ossian's Poems*, Philadelphia, 1794; Robert Treat Paine, *The Works in Prose and Verse of Robert Treat Paine Jun. Esq.*, Boston, 1812.

Cognizance was taken also of the enormous amount of ephemeral verse published in the periodicals of the time by examining the poetry in several of the best edited and most literary of the periodicals: *The Universal Asylum and Columbian Magazine* (Philadelphia, 1786-1792); *The Monthly Magazine and American Review* (New York, 1799-1800); the *Port Folio* (Philadelphia, 1801-1815); the *Monthly Anthology and Boston Review* (Boston, 1803-1811). Anthology verse was represented by *The Columbian Muse*, New York, 1794, though the verse here, as in most of the other anthologies of the time, consisted chiefly of excerpts from the major poets named above.

The greater part of the literary criticism of the early national period is to be found in the periodicals—especially those under the editorship of men of superior literary talents, such as Joseph Dennie's *Port Folio*, Charles Brockden Brown's *Monthly Magazine and American Review*, Matthew Carey's *Universal Asylum and Columbian Magazine*, though in addition to these the entire file of titles in the Early American Periodical Series published by University Microfilms, Ann Arbor, Michigan, was examined. Some criticism is also to be found in occasional volumes like Charles Prentiss' *A Collection of Fugitive Essays*, Leominster, Mass., 1797; or John Blair Linn's *Miscellaneous Works, Prose and Poetical*, New York, 1795. Some is to be found in addresses like John Trumbull's *Essay on the Use and Advantage of the Fine Arts . . .*, New Haven, 1770; some in prefaces, notes, and appended materials to poems such as

Thomas Green Fessenden's *Terrible Tractoration,* Boston, 1803; some in the verse itself of such poems as John Blair Linn's *The Powers of Genius . . .,* Philadelphia, 1802; some in pamphlets and published orations such as those in the seventy-nine volumes of Woolcott Pamphlets in the Rare Book Room of the Library of Congress; some in the prefaces and notes to American editions of the British poets; some in the dictionaries, encyclopedias, and grammars. But all these miscellaneous sources were found to add comparatively little to the main corpus of critical writing in the periodicals. Two titles falling outside the general limit of 1815 were found to be particularly valuable for general commentary on literary matters in the early national period: Samuel Kettell, *Specimens of American Poetry, With Critical and Biographical Notices,* Boston, 1829, 3 vols.; Samuel Knapp, *Lectures on American Literature . . .,* New York, 1829.

The following rhetorical texts, elocution manuals, readers, and critical treatises were of chief importance during the period: Hugh Blair, *Lectures on Rhetoric and Belles Lettres,* London, 1783; Henry Home, Lord Kames, *Elements of Criticism,* London, 1759, 2 vols.; James Burgh, *The Art of Speaking . . .,* London, 1761; George Campbell, *The Philosophy of Rhetoric,* Edinburgh, 1776; Thomas Sheridan, *A Discourse Being Introductory to His Course of Lectures on Elocution,* London, 1759; John Walker, *Elements of Elocution,* London, 1781; John Ward, *A System of Oratory,* London, 1759; John Quincy Adams, *Lectures on Rhetoric and Oratory,* Cambridge, Mass., 1810, 2 vols.; Noah Webster, *An American Selection of Lessons in Reading and Speaking . . .,* Boston, 1792; John Witherspoon, *Lectures on Moral Philosophy and Eloquence,* Philadelphia, 1810.

Many critics from the ancient world to modern times were perused in establishing workable distinctions between rhetoric and poetic. Among these were *Aristotle's Art of Poetry,* edited by W. Hamilton Fyfe, Oxford, 1940, and *The Rhetoric of Aristotle,* translated by Lane Cooper, New York, 1932; E. M. Cope, *An Introduction to Aristotle's Rhetoric,* London, 1867; Charles S. Baldwin, *Ancient Rhetoric and Poetic,* New York, 1924, and *Medieval Rhetoric and Poetic,* New York, 1928; Donald L. Clark, *Rhetoric and Poetry in the Renaissance,* New York, 1922; Cicero, *Brutus,* translated by G. L. Henrickson, Cambridge, Mass., 1931, *On Oratory and Orators [De Oratore],* translated and edited by William Guthrie, rev. ed., London, 1908, and *Orator,* translated by H. M. Hubbell, Cambridge, Mass., 1931; Horace, *Satires, Epistles,* and *Ars Poetica,* translated by H. Rushton Fairclough (1 vol.), New York, 1929; *Longinus on the Sublime,* translated by W. Rhys Roberts, Cambridge, 1907; John Stuart Mill, "Thoughts on Poetry and Its Varieties," in *Dissertations and Discussions,* New York, 1874, 2 vols.; Quintilian, *Institutio Oratoria,* translated by H. B. Butler, London, 1932, 4 vols. The following also proved valuable: for authoritative comment on epideictic discourse, Theodore C. Burgess, *Epideictic Literature,* in *University of Chicago Studies in Classical Philology,* III (1902), 89-261, and Edouard Norden, *Die Antike Kunstprosa,* Berlin, 1915; for historical surveys of rhetorical theory, Harold F. Harding, "English Rhetorical Theory, 1750-1800," unpublished dissertation, Cornell University, 1937, William P. Sandford, *English Theories of Public Address, 1530-1828,* Columbus, Ohio, 1929, and Warren A. Guthrie, "The Development of Rhetorical Theory in America, 1635-1850," unpublished dissertation, Northwestern University, 1940; for studies of the impact of the Scottish rhetoricians upon American poets and critics, William Charvat, *The Origins of American Critical Thought 1810-1835,* Philadelphia, 1936, and Leon Howard, *The Connecticut Wits,* Chicago, 1943.

UNIVERSITY OF FLORIDA MONOGRAPHS

Humanities

No. 1 (Spring 1959): *The Uncollected Letters of James Gates Percival*
Edited by Harry R. Warfel

No. 2 (Fall 1959): *Leigh Hunt's Autobiography The Earliest Sketches*
Edited by Stephen F. Fogle

No. 3 (Winter 1960): *Pause Patterns in Elizabethan and Jacobean Drama*
By Ants Oras

No. 4 (Spring 1960): *Rhetoric and American Poetry of the Early National Period*
By Gordon E. Bigelow